IT'S YOUR MONEY!

SIMPLE STRATEGIES TO MAXIMIZE YOUR SOCIAL SECURITY INCOME

It's Your Money!
Simple Strategies to Maximize Your Social Security Income

Windy City Publishers
2118 Plum Grove Rd., #349
Rolling Meadows, IL 60008
www.windycitypublishers.com

Published in the United States of America

10 9 8 7 6 5 4 3 2 1

First Edition: 2012

Library of Congress Control Number:
2012946154

ISBN:
978-1-935766-59-9

Windy City Publishers
CHICAGO

A NOTE FROM OUR ATTORNEYS

Please keep in mind that everyone's individual situation is unique. The information being presented is general and for educational purposes only; it may not apply to your specific circumstances. The material being presented may provide clues, but not necessarily answers for your specific situation and is presented with the intent of accuracy based on current law. Congress may change the law governing benefit amounts at any time.

The authors, or Social Security Central LLC, cannot be held responsible for any direct or incidental loss resulting from applying any of the information provided or from any other source mentioned. The information provided does not constitute any legal, tax or accounting advice.

This book is designed to help you confidently work with the Social Security Administration with regards to your Social Security benefits. To apply for your benefits, contact the Social Security Administration and work with them for a formal decision on your application.

TABLE OF CONTENTS

PART TWO
SOCIAL SECURITY CENTRAL LLC HELPS DEVELOP YOUR MAXIMIZATION STRATEGY

PART THREE
SOCIAL SECURITY CENTRAL LLC HELPS YOU FILE WITH THE SSA

Tee Time
An Introduction

Maury and Bob were golf partners for 47 years. Each year, as winter became spring, and the frost still lingered, the men began their weekly round of eighteen holes. They always played the same course, a few miles from home, and met just before their one o'clock tee time. One summer Saturday afternoon as they sat in the clubhouse polishing their irons, Bob breaks the silence, "I wonder if there's golf in heaven?" Maury responds with "I sure hope so! We've been playing together our whole lives. It'd be a shame for that to end." "Tell you what," Bob proposes, "let's make a deal. The first one of us that passes will come back and let the other know whether or not there's golf in heaven."

They shake hands to seal their quirky little deal and hit the links, just like they had every Saturday before. As life would have it, Bob passed away six months later. But, Maury kept up their Saturday afternoon golf tradition. He played the same course, a few miles from home, with a one o'clock tee time.

This continued week after week until one Saturday, sure enough, Bob was miraculously sitting in the corner of the clubhouse waiting for Maury to arrive.

"Holy cow! You're back!" Maury screams.

Bob replies, "We made a deal, didn't we?"

"Well, I got to know…is there golf in heaven?" asks Maury.

As promised, Bob delivers his report. "I've got some good news and some bad news. The good news: There is golf in heaven! The bad news: Your first tee time is next Tuesday."

Of course this joke takes a light-hearted look at the inevitability of life, but it does illustrate an important retirement consideration. How easy would it be to manage your retirement income if you knew your 'tee time'? What if you could spend your very last dollar in your very last hour? Wouldn't that be the ultimate retirement income plan?

Well of course, that's impossible. But there are other 'tee times' that you *can* plan for...collecting Social Security benefits. The decision of when to begin collecting your Social Security benefits is a decision that the majority of Americans will make during the transition into retirement. What most people don't realize is that the right decision can, in and of itself, significantly impact your retirement lifestyle.

The rules of retirement are being rewritten by an aging generation of thinkers, innovators, and trailblazers. Baby boomers—the flower-powered, free-loving, tie-dyed shirt wearing kids that sparked a cultural revolution in the 1960s—are now turning age 60 at a rate of 10,000 per day! They're bringing their bold, creative, establishment-bucking thinking into retirement and trading their parents' retirement rocking chairs to start retirement rock bands. Not content with just sitting around in their golden years, baby boomers are embracing retirement not as an ending, but as a new start.

More and more, baby boomers head towards retirement with plans of exotic travel, retirement homes, new cars, spa treatments and 4-star meals— pleasures their parents and grandparents never considered.

For this new generation, retirement doesn't necessarily mean the end of a paycheck either. While many will retire from their current career or jobs, many will continue on to a new career or role they find more rewarding, fulfilling and passion-driven. This new venture often means less full-time work and a better balance between work and play.

However, retirees are facing new challenges. The good news is—thanks to developments in science and medicine, exercise and diet, occupations and lifestyle—we're living longer. In fact, for an American couple both age 65 there is a 50% chance that one will live to age 92 and a 25% chance that one will live to age 97. The bottom line is that most of us will have to plan for a three-decade retirement. Of course, the longer we live, the more money we need for financial dignity and financial independence during retirement.

The sources of retirement income are changing. In generations past, many Americans got a monthly pension check that provided a steady source of retirement income. Today, most of us will have to provide our own retirement check from individual and, possibly, employer-sponsored savings programs. This creates a whole new set of financial risks tied to personal investments, inflation, interest rates, market performance, and inevitably, the real possibility of running out of retirement income.

The one connection between yesterday's retirement and today's is Social Security. The spirit of Social Security not only endures, but the role of Social Security has never been more important. For many of us, Social Security may be the only source of guaranteed, inflation protected, lifetime income. Yet the majority of Americans don't understand what their Social Security benefits are, when they should collect them, and the strategies on how to maximize their cumulative lifetime monthly Social Security benefits.

Over the last 70 years though, the Social Security system has continued to increase in complexity. It has been amended, expanded and reformed to the point where most Americans have no idea whether they are truly maximizing the monthly benefits they've earned throughout their working years. As a result, many retirees make wrong decisions costing thousands of dollars in lost lifetime income when they may need it most.

This book from Social Security Central LLC aims to give you confidence in deciding when to begin collecting Social Security and clarity that you are truly maximizing your cumulative lifetime benefits.

You've paid into Social Security for years. Don't you owe it to yourself to maximize your benefits when the time comes? IT'S YOUR MONEY!

PART ONE

Social Security Central LLC
Answers Your Questions

Simply put, Social Security Central LLC wants to help you maximize your Social Security benefits. Unfortunately, over the last 70 plus years the Social Security system has only increased in complexity. It has been amended, expanded, and reformed to the point where most of us have no idea if we are truly maximizing the benefits we are eligible for, paid into, and earned through our working years. As a result, the majority of Americans end up making wrong decisions about their Social Security benefits costing them thousands of dollars.

If the idea of Social Security makes your head spin, you're not alone. The Social Security Administration (SSA) reports over 850,000 weekly visitors to their offices and more than 68 million phone calls a year!

The goal of Social Security Central LLC is not to make you an expert on Social Security. With endless nuances and countless permutations of payout scenarios, it would take a lifetime of education. Plus, you have free unlimited access to the experts at the Social Security Administration Office. With hundreds of local offices, a telephone hotline and a comprehensive website, these government resources are always at your disposal.

But it is important to understand what the Social Security Administration (SSA) officials are experts on. They are experts on answering your questions, not giving advice. Nobody with the SSA is paid or compensated to give you advice or ensure that you are making the right decisions and maximizing the benefits. After all, you've paid into the system for years. IT'S YOUR MONEY!

Again, we don't want to make you an expert, but we do want to provide you with a suite of tools, including our proprietary Benefit Maximization Calculator (at www.socialsecuritycentral.com), that can help maximize your Social Security benefits. This includes answering common questions like: When can I or when should I take my Social Security benefit? How do I calculate my Full Retirement Age (FRA)? How do I calculate an estimate of my monthly benefit? What are spousal benefits? What is a survivor benefit? Most importantly, am I maximizing my total Social Security benefits?

We ultimately want you to be fully prepared when you file for your Social Security benefits with the Social Security Administration.

1 Thanks, FDR

How It All Began and How It Keeps Going

To understand America's commitment to future generations, it is important to look at the peace of mind Social Security provided to past generations.

The Social Security Act was written into law during the backdrop of the Great Depression and signed by President Franklin D. Roosevelt on August 14, 1935 as part of FDR's New Deal. It was created to protect what were seen as dangers in the "modern American" life: old age, poverty, unemployment, and the burdens of widows and fatherless children. Think of it as a financial safety net. It promised the American people "some measure of protection against the loss of a job and against poverty-ridden old age."

Social Security is a social insurance program that is primarily funded through dedicated payroll taxes called Federal Insurance Contributions Act (FICA). It is the largest government program of its type in the world as measured in dollars and is one of the single greatest expenditures in the federal budget. Even though it was written into law in 1935, payroll taxes weren't collected to pay for the system until 1937. Originally, you had the choice of taking a lump sum or monthly payout. In the first 3 years, everyone took the lump sum, with Ernest Ackerman being the first American to receive a lump sum payment in 1937. He received a total of 17 cents and had paid 5 cents into the program. The first monthly check was issued in January of 1940 to Ida May Fuller of Ludlow, VT. She is also the first American who truly maximized the value of her Social Security benefit. She paid a total of $24.75 into the system for 3 years, 1937, 1938 and 1939. The first monthly payment she received was for $22.54, and by her second check she had already received more out of Social Security than she had paid into the system. Any guess on how long Ida May lived for?

Let me give you a hint. In the 1930s, if you lived until 60 you were doing pretty well. In fact, life expectancy in 1930 was only 58 for men and 62 for women. Miss Fuller actually lived to be 100 years old and maximized her benefits by choosing the monthly payout. Over her lifetime, she collected just under $23,000 in total Social Security benefits having contributed only $24.75 - a return of over 92,000%! It's a wonderful story (posted on www. ssa.gov), but also highlights the importance of understanding how you can maximize your Social Security benefits. Just think, what if Ida May had taken the lump-sum payout?

Many American's believe that for a myriad of reasons, Social Security is going bust very quickly. Much of the information that your have read or heard about regarding the lack of solvency in the near term is simply bad information. The current long-term financial condition of the Social Security program remains challenging and will require legislative modifications due to substantial cost growth in the upcoming decades. This is the result of an aging population (we are living longer) and fewer workers per retiree paying into the system. However, the 2012 report on the status of Social Security and Medicare Programs by the Board of Trustees who oversee the fund found that if left alone, the Social Security Trust Fund will be able to pay all benefits though 2021 simply from the interest earned on the fund itself. After 2021, tapping both principal and interest from the fund will support and pay all scheduled benefits as is through 2033. Thereafter, collected receipts from income tax (FICA) would be able to pay 75% of current benefits through 2086. While the Social Security system will need legislative change to avoid its long-term financial challenges and potential to disrupt payments for today's young workforce, the summary by the fund's trustees found that it currently satisfies the conditions for short-term financial adequacy.

Social Security is not going broke. Taking your monthly benefit early out of fear may cost you and your family thousands of dollars in retirement.

By law, the trustees are required to publish a current status summary of the Social Security and Medicare programs and make a 75-year long-term forecast of the program. The need to reform the system is nothing new. In fact, there have been many modifications to the system over the years to ensure its solvency. The first changes to Social Security were made back in 1939, four years after it was signed into law. Back then, one reason sited for the changes was the growing concern over the impact that payroll taxes were having on the economy. The payroll taxes were even partially blamed for the Recession of 1937. Sound familiar? During the early 1980s, the Reagan administration along with Congress made several controversial changes, including: raising the amount that employers and workers contributed, gradually increasing the Full Retirement Age (FRA) from 65 to age 67, and creating the idea of "means testing" by making Social Security benefits taxable for higher-income individuals. As a result, the Social Security system began to generate surplus funds designed to cover the added costs of the baby boomers. President Reagan summarized these needed changes by stating, "Social Security assures the elderly that America will always keep the promises made in troubled times a half century ago." To insure the long-term promise of Social Security, we join others in acknowledging a need to make changes to the current system including, raising the FRA, raising payroll taxes, and diversifying the Social Security Trust Fund. However, none of these changes would have a material affect for Americans 55 and older according to the experts[1]. This is the viewpoint used for constructing the strategies in this book.

---

1   Boston College's Center for Retirement Research

Bottom line, claiming your Social Security benefits early because you think the system is going broke and you won't get your money is a **poor decision**. Furthermore, it is an uninformed and uneducated decision, yet has remained a mindset since the early days of the program. Claiming early can cost you and your family thousands of needed retirement dollars and will not allow you to maximize the benefits you worked hard for so many years to earn. Think if in 1940 Ida May Fuller took a lump sum based out of fear instead of the monthly lifetime check she continued to receive until she passed away in 1975 at age 100!

2 Ch... Ch... Ch... Changes

Social Security: Yesterday v. Today

Social Security is one of the largest and more complicated retirement assets. Almost all Americans are eligible, but very few retirees receive any guidance on how to properly maximize their benefits.

The Social Security benefit that you have paid into your entire working years is designed to be a supplemental source of retirement income to help you keep your financial dignity and independence in retirement. It may also be one of the most confusing programs costing you thousands of dollars during your golden years without proper planning. For millions of Americans, Social Security is the foundation of their retirement income plan, providing up to half of their income. More than likely it offers one of the only sources of lifetime, inflation adjusted income you can count on.

> For millions of Americans, Social Security is the foundation of their retirement plan, providing up to half of their income.

Looking back, didn't your parent's generation make retirement look easy? They collected their pension check, collected their Social Security, and made up for any shortfalls with the interest income from their savings. Americans today have little confidence in their ability to afford a comfortable lifestyle in retirement because today's retirement looks very different from a generation or two ago. Different not just from a longevity standpoint, but the sources of retirement income have changed as well.

The Boston College Center for Retirement Research estimates that the number of employees covered by a defined benefit retirement plan (the ones we think of as traditional pension plans) declined from 62% in 1983 to 17% in 2010. Most of us will have to fund our retirement with income from our own individual and employer-sponsored savings like 401k(s), IRAs, Simple Plans, etc. This self-funded retirement becomes even more challenging in today's savings and investing environment characterized by above average unemployment, low interest rates and high volatility in global stock markets.

Most of these plans do provide investment options that allow you, the participant, to diversify across many different types of investments from conservative to aggressive. They provide you with the freedom to take a lump sum or borrow against it. These programs often times allow for tax-deferral of the investment earnings and growth as well as providing for cash flow flexibility to take more or less income and to start or stop the income all together.

However, these retirement savings vehicles come with many risks that need to be carefully managed. They are subject to market risk which cause the value of the accounts to fluctuate as markets move up and down. Market cycles are difficult to predict and can be challenging to manage without proper guidance and diversification. Retiring into a down or negative market could mean less money is available in your accounts due to market losses. Of course the less money in your individual retirement accounts, the less income those accounts will generate for you and your spouse to live off of in retirement.

Individual retirement accounts rarely provide a steady, monthly, lifetime income like the pension plans of yester-year, and there is a possibility that the income may run out without careful planning. This risk, sometimes referred to as sequence of return risk, causes your income to run out quicker than anticipated. For example, if you are taking a 5% income stream from your IRA to live off of in retirement (a monthly systematic withdrawal) and your IRA account is earning 8% (net of all fees) every year, then your account value is earning more than you are withdrawing. This positive situation would result in a slight increase in your account value every year and increase the likelihood that your assets will be large enough to generate a monthly retirement income for many years to come. However, if you are taking that same 5% monthly systematic withdrawal from your IRA to live off of in retirement and the account is earning 0% (net of fees) or less, the IRA account is now losing value. If these losses occur early in your retirement and continue for a period of time (like the financial crisis of 2008 and the low interest rate environment that followed), there is a significant likelihood that you will deplete your retirement assets and run out of retirement income. These are just some of the new risks that we face with today's modern retirement.

The good news is that one connection between yesterday's retirement and today's retirement is Social Security. The spirit of Social Security not only survives today, but the role of Social Security has never been more important. For most of us, Social Security may be the only source of lifetime inflation adjusted income to help us meet our essential retirement living expenses. So we challenge you to look at this important retirement asset, a system we have paid into our entire working years, more closely. It's important that we understand the thousands of dollars we may be costing ourselves, our spouses, and even our children by simply taking Social Security benefits as early as we can.

If you count yourself among the majority of baby boomers who fear outliving their money more than they fear death, it's time to break with American tradition. More than two-thirds of Americans claim their Social Security benefit before they reach their Full Retirement Age (FRA), effectively denying themselves payouts that could be more than 75 percent higher if they just waited a bit longer to starting collecting. If you're looking to boost your retirement income, it's time for a major rethink on when to claim Social Security. Reading this book and taking five minutes with the proprietary Benefit Maximization Calculator from Social Security Central LLC is a great first step in maximizing your retirement income (www.socialsecuritycentral.com).

More than two-thirds of Americans claim their Social Security benefit before they reach their Full Retirement Age, effectively denying themselves payouts that could be more than 75 percent higher if they just waited a bit longer to starting collecting.

3 SPEAKING 'SOCIAL SECURITY'

DEFINING 12 IMPORTANT TERMS

"Your Primary Insurance Amount will depend on your Full Retirement Age along with your AIME which could include bend points and could be taxable based on your Provisional Income."

"I'm sorry, I don't speak Social Security. Could you please repeat that in English?"

Part of the reason that Social Security is so complicated and why millions of Americans leave thousand of dollars of benefits on the table is that the Social Security program has unique terms, words, and acronyms that we just don't understand.

In order to properly maximize your benefits, it is important to have an understanding of a few key words and terms. For most, this may feel a bit like learning a foreign language, but it is necessary for you to understand these key terms in creating your personal income maximization strategy. While there are even more terms and acronyms used for specific situations, we are going to cover the most frequently used.

1. FULL RETIREMENT AGE (FRA)

This is the age at which you would receive your full retirement benefit from Social Security. If you take your benefit prior to this age, your benefits and survivor benefits may be reduced. If you take your individual benefits after this age, you may receive more monthly income. Age 65 was the original Full Retirement Age (FRA) and is gradually increasing to age 67 based on year of birth. See Full Retirement Age Table below. Please note the widow/er survivor FRA is slightly different than the individual FRA (see Survivor Full Retirement Age Table under Survivor Benefits in this chapter). FRA is very important to understand since it is a primary determinant in how to maximize your Social Security benefit.

Full Retirement Age (FRA)	
Note: If you qualify for benefits as a survivor (widow/widower) your full retirement age may be different.	
Year of Birth*	**Full Retirement Age**
1937 or earlier	65
1938	65 and 2 months
1939	65 and 4 months
1940	65 and 6 months
1941	65 and 8 months
1942	65 and 10 months
1943-1954	66
1955	66 and 2 months
1956	66 and 4 months
1957	66 and 6 months
1958	66 and 8 months
1959	66 and 10 months
1960 and later	67
*If you were born on January 1st of any year you should refer to the previous year. (If you were born on the 1st of the month, we figure your benefit (and your full retirement age) as if your birthday was in the previous month.)	

Source: www.socialsecurity.gov/retire2/agereduction.htm

2. AVERAGE INDEXED MONTHLY EARNINGS (AIME)

This is your individual historical earnings (wages and self-employment income) used to collect taxes to pay into the Social Security system. Average Indexed Monthly Earnings (AIME) is calculated by looking at the average of the highest 35 years of earnings. Those earnings are added up and divided by 420 (35 years x 12 months). Earnings for each year before your individual age of 60 are indexed for inflation, in other words, increased to reflect what the equivalent wages would be in 'today's' dollars. For example, if you were born in 1950 and your wages in 1969 were $5600, they would be indexed or considered to be approximately $40,000 in 'today's' dollars when your benefits are computed. If you have not worked for 35 years, zeros will be added and factored in to calculate your AIME. Once your AIME is calculated, it will then be applied to a formula designed by the Social Security Administration (SSA) to determine your Primary Insurance Amount (PIA) or what you will receive on a monthly basis at Full Retirement Age (FRA). This formula (in the 2013 Primary Insurance Amount Calculation Table below PIA definition) is designed in the spirit of Social Security and will replace a greater percentage of lower wage workers/retirees income than it would a higher wager earner.

It is important to review your individual summary of earnings history with the Social Security Administration (SSA). The summary of your individual earnings can be found on your Social Security statement. Please note that the SSA suspended the annual mailing of the statement to taxpayers in March 2011. The SSA has made the statements available online for all workers and you can print the statement out. Simply go to www.ssa.gov and click on the link "*Get Your Social Security Statement Online*". You will need to register with a username and password and verify some information online before you have access; this should only take about 5 minutes. You can also go to your local Social Security office to request a Summary Earnings Query (SEQY) (or a Detailed Earnings Query (DEQY) that breaks down earnings and employer names from 1978 to present). Review your earnings record and check it for accuracy. There are millions of W-2s that are not credited to any taxpayer or recorded to the wrong taxpayer. The SSA will correct any errors or omissions of earnings once you provide the proper documentation.

3. Primary Insurance Amount (PIA)/Individual Benefit

This is the monthly Social Security benefit that you will receive at your individual Full Retirement Age (FRA). Your Primary Insurance Amount (PIA) is based on an in-depth calculation that will factor in your Average Indexed Monthly Earnings (AIME) as well as the maximum income subject to Social Security taxes. In general, your PIA may go down if you take your Social Security benefit before FRA and your monthly benefit may go up if you take your benefits after FRA. In addition, your spousal/ex-spousal, widow/er, disability and child benefits will all be based off your individual PIA. These amounts may be more or less than your individual PIA as we will later learn. You can find your estimated PIA on your Social Security statement. Again, the Social Security Administration (SSA) suspended the annual mailing of the statement to taxpayers in March 2011 and has made the statements available online for all workers. You can also find your PIA by logging into the retirement estimator on the SSA website at www.ssa.gov and clicking on the link "*Estimate Your Retirement Benefits*".

2013 Primary Insurance Amount (PIA) Calculation	
AIME	**PIA** (as % of AIME)
$0-791	90%
$791-4,768	$711.90 + 32% of the excess over $791
$4,768+	$1,984.54 + 15% of the excess over $4,768

Source: www.socialsecurity.gov/OACT/COLA/piaformula.html

4. Federal Insurance Contributions Act (FICA) Tax

The Federal Insurance Contributions Act (FICA) tax is a U.S. payroll tax or employment tax withheld from each paycheck, or paid by individuals and employers, as mandated by the Act to fund Social Security and Medicare. Generally, the employee taxes are collected at a rate of 7.65% applied to gross earnings with 6.2% for Social Security and 1.45% for Medicare. These rates have been lowered temporarily at times. For example, the Social Security tax rate in 2011 (extended into part of 2012) for individuals was lowered by 2% from 6.2% to 4.2%. The tax is only applied to a limited amount of earnings. The taxable earnings base limit in 2013 is $113,700 or a maximum Social Security contribution of $7049.40. *Note: This is not tax advice or tax planning, but simply a publication of current policy. Consult with a tax advisor for further information.*

When an individual worker pays Federal Income Contribution Act (FICA) taxes, you earn 'credits' toward your Social Security benefit eligibility. Individual earnings required to earn one credit in 2013 is $1160 and an individual can earn up to 4 credits per year. Once you earn 40 credits (approximately 10 years) you are considered to be fully insured, or eligible for Social Security benefits. Disability may be earned with fewer credits. It is important to note that attaining 40 credits DOES NOT mean that you will receive the highest Social Security monthly benefit or payout. It simply means that you are eligible, or have qualified for your Social Security benefit.

2013 FICA Limits & Earnings Credit	
Taxable Earnings Base	$113,700
Earnings Required to Earn One Credit	$1,160

Source: www.ssa.gov/policy/docs/quickfacts/prog_highlights/index.html

5. Social Security Administration (SSA)

The Social Security Administration (SSA) is an independent agency of the federal government that administers Social Security and Supplemental Security Income (SSI) as well as determines initial eligibility of Medicare. The central SSA office is located in Woodlawn, Maryland, but there are also 10 regional offices, 8 processing centers, and approximately 1300 field offices. The national toll-free telephone number is 1-800-772-1213 and can usually direct you to information from 7am to 7pm, Monday through Friday. The official website of the United States SSA is www.ssa.gov. This website is an excellent source of information, including forms, informational papers and a Retirement Estimator calculator. You can also apply for benefits online. Please keep in mind that service and claims representatives of the SSA are typically not allowed to provide advice nor have the tools to maximize your benefits. They are there to answer questions and provide information. Our goal at Social Security Central LLC is to provide you with the right questions and tools, including our proprietary Benefit Maximization Calculator, to be fully prepared to maximize your benefits when you decide to apply.

6. Summary Earnings Query (SEQY)

Summary Earnings Query (SEQY) is a summary of an individual's Social Security wage history that can be obtained from the Social Security Administration (SSA). Since 2011 the wage history summaries are no longer mailed annually. You can either get your earnings summary online at www.ssa.gov (click on the link "*Get Your Social Security Statement Online*"), or you can request a SEQY from your local Social Security office. The information will only be provided for the wage earner, and there is no charge to obtain the printed format. No appointment is necessary, but you will need proper identification: driver's license, state identification card, or U.S. passport. You should obtain this prior to applying for benefits so you can verify that your individual earnings history is correct, and properly maximize the income from your Social Security benefit. Individuals should ask for a "SEQY printout" and if need be ask for a supervisor or reference the Social Security procedures manual Section GN 03311.005 F.2.a.

7. Cost of Living Adjustment (COLA)

Social Security benefits are automatically increased each year based on the percentage increase in the Consumer Price Index for Urban Wage Earners and Clerical Earners (CPI-W). The CPI-W is determined by the Bureau of Labor Statistics. The purpose of a Cost of Living Adjustment (COLA) is to ensure that the purchasing power of Social Security benefits is not eroded by the rising costs of goods or services. Congress enacted the COLA provision in a 1972 amendment and automatic COLA increases began in 1975. As seen in the table below, the COLA in 2010 and 2011 was 0%, but in 2012 the COLA was 3.6% and therefore automatically increased Social Security benefit payouts.

Historical Cost of Living Adjustments (COLAs)			
Automatic Cost Of Living Adjustments			
July 1975	-- 8.0%	January 1995	-- 2.8%
July 1976	-- 6.4%	January 1996	-- 2.6%
July 1977	-- 5.9%	January 1997	-- 2.9%
July 1978	-- 6.5%	January 1998	-- 2.1%
July 1979	-- 9.9%	January 1999	-- 1.3%
July 1980	-- 14.3%	January 2000	-- 2.5%[1]
July 1981	-- 11.2%	January 2001	-- 3.5%
July 1982	-- 7.4%	January 2002	-- 2.6%
January 1984	-- 3.5%	January 2003	-- 1.4%
January 1985	-- 3.5%	January 2004	-- 2.1%
January 1986	-- 3.1%	January 2005	-- 2.7%
January 1987	-- 1.3%	January 2006	-- 4.1%
January 1988	-- 4.2%	January 2007	-- 3.3%
January 1989	-- 4.0%	January 2008	-- 2.3%
January 1990	-- 4.7%	January 2009	-- 5.8%
January 1991	-- 5.4%	January 2010	-- 0.0%
January 1992	-- 3.7%	January 2011	-- 0.0%
January 1993	-- 3.0%	January 2012	-- 3.6%
January 1994	-- 2.6%	January 2013	--1.7%

[1] *The COLA for December 1999 was originally determined as 2.4 percent based on CPIs published by the Bureau of Labor Statistics. Pursuant to Public Law 106-554, however, this COLA is effectively now 2.5 percent.*

Source: www.ssa.gov/cola/automatic-cola.htm

8. Delayed Retirement Credit (DRC)

A Delayed Retirement Credit (DRC) is an increase or 'bonus' of up to 8% per year that is added to your monthly benefits for every month you wait to take your Social Security benefit after you turn your individual Full Retirement Age (FRA). This increase is in addition to the Cost Of Living Adjustment (COLA) applied each year. Delayed Retirement Credits (DRCs) are calculated monthly and depend on the year you were born. DRCs apply to every month you wait to take benefits past your FRA up to age 70. These monthly credits only apply to the individual benefit or a survivor benefit and have no impact on a spousal benefit. DRCs are an important way to maximize your potential total Social Security benefits.

9. Spousal Benefits/Ex-Spousal Benefits

Spousal/ex-spousal benefits are a monthly benefit based on an eligible individual's earnings history payable to an eligible spouse/ex-spouse of that individual. A spouse/ex-spouse does not need to be eligible for an individual benefit in order to receive a monthly spousal benefit. However, there are certain requirements that a spouse needs to meet in order to become eligible: spouse is at least age 62 and married for at least 1 year; OR spouse (any age) is caring for a child under age 16; OR spouse is at least age 50 and disabled. The spousal benefit can be as much as half of the worker's Primary Insurance Amount (PIA) depending on the spouse's age when applying for the benefit. An ex-spouse may be eligible for a spousal benefit even if the spouse has not filed for benefits if the following conditions are met: ex-spouse is at least age 62, marriage lasted at least 10 years and divorce occurred 2 or more years ago; OR ex-spouse (any age) is caring for a child age under 16; OR ex-spouse is at least age 50 and disabled. For couples, understanding the spousal benefit and the ways to collect it are important ways to maximize your potential total Social Security benefits.

10. Survivor Benefits

Survivor benefits are a monthly benefit based on an eligible individual's earnings history payable to an eligible surviving spouse/ex-spouse of that individual. Recipients of a survivor benefit do not have to be eligible for their own individual benefit. A widow/er is eligible for a survivor benefit if he/she is at least age 60 and married for at least 9 months. The length of marriage requirement is waived if the widow/er is caring for a child of the deceased spouse and the child is under age 16. The survivor benefit also applies if the survivor is at least age 50 and disabled. The survivor benefit can be as much as the deceased worker's Primary Insurance Amount (PIA) depending on the spouse's age when applying for the benefit. Survivor benefits may also receive Delayed Retirement Credits (DRCs) in certain situations, resulting in a bigger monthly income. Your Full Retirement Age (FRA) for a survivor benefit is slightly different than your Full Retirement Age for your own individual benefit. If you take your survivor benefit prior to this age, it may be reduced. See Survivor Full Retirement Age Table below. For couples, widows and widowers, understanding the survivor benefit and the ways to collect it are important ways to maximize your potential total Social Security benefits.

		Survivor Full Retirement Age (FRA)		
Year of Birth[1]	Full (survivors) Retirement Age[2]	At age 62 [3] a $1000 survivors benefit would be reduced to	Months between age 60 and full retirement age	Monthly % reduction [4]
1939 or earlier	65	$829	60	.475
1940	65 and 2 months	$825	62	.460
1941	65 and 4 months	$822	64	.445
1942	65 and 6 months	$819	66	.432
1943	65 and 8 months	$816	68	.419
1944	65 and 10 months	$813	70	.407
1945-1956	66	$810	72	.396
1957	66 and 2 months	$807	74	.385
1958	66 and 4 months	$805	76	.375
1959	66 and 6 months	$803	78	.365
1960	66 and 8 months	$801	80	.356
1961	66 and 10 months	$798	82	.348
1962 and later	67	$796	84	.339

(1) If the survivor was born on January 1st of any year, use the information for the previous year.

(2) If someone was born on the 1st of the month, we figure the benefit (and the full retirement age) as if his or her birthday was in the previous month. **Note:** The full retirement age may be different for retirement benefits.

(3) The $1000 benefit would be reduced to $715 for anyone who started receiving survivors benefits at age 60.

(5) Monthly reduction percentages are approximate due to rounding. The maximum benefit is limited to what the worker would receive if he or she were still alive. Survivors benefits that start at age 60 are always reduced by 28.50%.

Source: www.socialsecurity.gov/survivorplan/survivorchartred.htm

11. Disability Benefits

Disability benefits are a monthly benefit based on an eligible individual's earnings history in which the individual is severely impaired—physically or mentally—and are not able to perform any substantial gainful activity. The medical conditions need to last at least one year or result in death. Disability benefits can come from both the Social Security program as well as the Social Security's Supplemental Security Income (SSI) program. The number of work credits needed for disability benefits depends on the age at which the individual becomes disabled. Individuals younger than age 62 may be eligible with less than 40 Social Security credits. In addition, there may be a waiting period before receiving disability benefits.

Credits Needed to Qualify for Disability Benefits	
Unless you are blind, you must have earned at least 20 of the credits in the 10 years immediately before you became disabled.	
Born after 1929, Became Disabled at Age	**Number of Credits You Need**
31 - 42	20
44	22
46	24
48	26
50	28
52	30
54	32
56	34
58	36
60	38
62 or older	40

Source: www.socialsecurity.gov/retire2/credits3.htm

12. Children's Benefits

Children's benefits are a monthly benefit based on an eligible individual's earnings history who has filed for retirement, disability or passed away that is made payable to their child who is unmarried and under age 18 (if still in high school up to age 19). Unmarried children that are disabled before age 22 may also qualify. Children may only collect on one parent's work history. Children are eligible to receive benefits up to 50% of the parent's Primary Insurance Amount (PIA) if the parent is still alive and up to 75% of a deceased parent's PIA. Benefits usually terminate at the child's age of 18 or if the disability ends.

4 Just the Facts, Ma'm

Who? When? What If? How Much? How Long?

Who Is Eligible and When?

In order to be eligible for your Social Security monthly benefit, you need to have worked for approximately 10 years, be at least age 62, and a U.S. citizen (or legal alien).

Most Americans pay payroll taxes as mandated by the Federal Insurance Contributions Act (FICA). Generally, the employee taxes are collected at a rate of 7.65% applied to gross earnings with 6.2% for Social Security and 1.45% for Medicare. These rates have been lowered temporarily at times. For example, the Social Security tax rate in 2011 (and extended into part of 2012) for individuals was lowered by 2% from 6.2% to 4.2%. The FICA tax is only applied to a limited amount of earnings. The taxable earnings base limit in 2013 is $113,700 or a maximum Social Security contribution of $7049.40. *Note: This is not tax advice or tax planning, but simply a publication of current policy. Please consult with a tax advisor for further information.*

When an individual worker pays FICA taxes, you earn "credits" toward your Social Security benefit eligibility. Individual earnings required to earn one credit in 2013 is $1160 and an individual can earn up to 4 credits per year. Once you earn 40 credits (approximately 10 years) you are considered to be fully insured or eligible for Social Security benefits. Disability may be earned with fewer credits. It is important to note that attaining 40 credits DOES NOT mean that you will receive the highest Social Security monthly benefit or payout. It simply means that you are eligible or have qualified for your Social Security benefit.

So once you are eligible or are considered "fully insured" for your Social Security monthly benefit, when can you begin to receive payments? Your Full Retirement Age (FRA) is the age at which you would receive your full retirement benefit from Social Security. Age 65 was the original FRA and is gradually being increased to age 67 based on the year you were born. Most Americans claiming Social Security benefits today have an FRA of 66. See Full Retirement Age Table below. Please note the widow/er survivor FRA is slightly different than the individual FRA (see Survivor Full Retirement Age Table under Survivor Benefits in Chapter 3). FRA is a very important age to understand since it is a primary determinant in how to maximize your Social Security benefit.

Full Retirement Age (FRA)

Note: If you qualify for benefits as a survivor (widow/widower) your full retirement age may be different.

Year of Birth*	Full Retirement Age
1937 or earlier	65
1938	65 and 2 months
1939	65 and 4 months
1940	65 and 6 months
1941	65 and 8 months
1942	65 and 10 months
1943-1954	66
1955	66 and 2 months
1956	66 and 4 months
1957	66 and 6 months
1958	66 and 8 months
1959	66 and 10 months
1960 and later	67

*If you were born on January 1st of any year you should refer to the previous year. (If you were born on the 1st of the month, we figure your benefit (and your full retirement age) as if your birthday was in the previous month.)

Source: www.socialsecurity.gov/retire2/agereduction.htm

You can actually begin to receive your monthly Social Security income beginning at age 62, well before your Full Retirement Age (FRA). However, you are not considered to be at your FRA and as a result, your monthly benefit and survivor benefits may be permanently reduced. The reduction in monthly income for taking the Social Security benefit before FRA is a percentage reduction for each month the benefit is taken prior to FRA. The monthly reduction is 5/9% for every month you claimed the benefit early within 36 months of your FRA. If the monthly benefit was claimed 37-60 months prior to your FRA, an additional 5/12% per month reduction will be applied for each additional month beyond 3 years prior to FRA. Let's make some sense of this math. If your FRA is 66 and you collect benefits at age 62 and 6 months, your benefits will be reduced by 22.5%. Here's how we come up with that: (5/9% x 36 months) = 20%, (5/12% x 6 months) = 2.5%, (20% + 2.5%) = 22.5% in total monthly benefit permanent reduction. Bottom line, if you take your monthly Social Security benefit prior to your FRA, your benefits will be permanently reduced!

% Individual Benefits Received if Collected Early						
	Age of Collection					
FRA	62	63	64	65	66	67
65	80%	86.7%	93.3%	100%	--	--
66	75%	80%	86.7%	93.3%	100%	--
67	70%	75%	80%	86.7%	93.3%	100%

Source: www.socialsecurity.gov/retire2/agereduction.htm

If you wait to claim your Social Security benefits after your Full Retirement Age (FRA), your monthly benefits will permanently increase in value for each month you delay receiving your monthly income up to age 70. This is a bonus added to your monthly benefit and is called a Delayed Retirement Credit (DRC). The increase in your monthly benefit is 2/3% for each month or 8% for each year you delay past your FRA until age 70. Are your other retirement investments earning you more than 8%? For example, if your FRA is 66 and you wait to claim your monthly benefit until age 68 you will increase your monthly Social Security benefit by 16%. (2/3% x 24 months) = 16%. The maximum bonus or increase (DRCs) you are eligible to receive in your monthly payout is a 32% increase; achieved by waiting until age 70. Bottom line, the longer you wait to take your monthly Social Security benefit, the higher your monthly benefit will permanently be. Check out the difference below of a $1000 benefit at Full Retirement Age (FRA) of 66, if taken early and if postponed to age 70.

Are your other retirement investments earning you more than 8%? Your monthly Social Security benefit may increase up to 8% each year you delay collection past your Full Retirement Age until age 70.

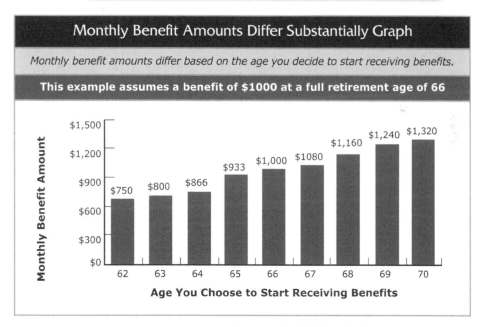

Source: www.socialsecurity.gov/pubs/10147.html#a0=1

Note: Many people assume that Social Security benefits may only be taken at 3 ages (62, FRA & 70); however, benefits can be taken any year or month between 62 and 70 (with few exceptions). As discussed above, a number of months can make a difference in your benefit amount.

WHAT IF I CHANGE MY MIND AFTER COLLECTING MY BENEFITS?

You may withdraw your decision to collect monthly Social Security benefits within the first year of filing for benefits.

Life happens and in some cases, you may regret your decision to collect your monthly Social Security benefits, especially if you decided to collect benefits early. Maybe you decided to go back to work shortly after collecting benefits. Perhaps you unexpectedly came across an inheritance and you plan to live off the newfound money and would like to allow your monthly Social Security benefit to grow from Delayed Retirement Credits (DRCs). Or you simply made a poor decision prior to knowing how to maximize your benefits.

The Social Security Administration (SSA) provides you with some flexibility if you have a change of heart in your decision to take benefits for whatever reason. You are allowed to file a Request for Withdrawal of Application form with the Social Security Administration within the first 12 months of collecting monthly Social Security benefits. You are only allowed to file once per lifetime. If the SSA grants approval of your request, you need to repay all benefits received back to the SSA. The amount repaid must include your total individual benefits received, total benefits that may have gone to a spouse or other dependent, and any money withheld such as Medicare premiums and tax withholding. You are not responsible for any interest or penalties. You are then able to re-file for monthly Social Security benefits at a future date.

HOW MUCH CAN I GET?

Your actual monthly Social Security benefit will be based on how old you are when you start to collect it and the average of your highest 35 years of earnings on which you you've paid payroll taxes into Social Security. All Social Security monthly benefits are derived from your Primary Insurance Amount (PIA). This is the monthly Social Security benefit that you will receive at your individual Full Retirement Age (FRA) as previously discussed. Your PIA is based on an in-depth calculation that will factor in your Average Indexed Monthly Earnings (AIME) as well as the maximum income subject to Social Security taxes. This is your individual historical earnings (wages and self-employment income) used to collect taxes to pay into the Social Security system. The cap or limit on how much income that will be subject to FICA tax is currently $113,700 (in 2013). Any income that you earn above this amount is not currently taxed for Social Security purposes. Your AIME is calculated by looking at the average of the highest 35 years of earnings. Those earnings are added up and divided by 420 (35 years x 12 months). Earnings for each year before your individual age of 60 are indexed for inflation or increased to reflect what the equivalent wages would be in 'today's' dollars. For example, if you were born in 1950 and your wages in 1969 were $5600, they would be indexed or considered to be approximately $40,000 in 'today's' dollars when your benefits are computed. If you have not worked for 35 years, zeros will be added and factored in to calculate your AIME. You can still increase your benefits for wages earned after starting Social Security benefits, provided that the most recent yearly wages are included in the highest 35 years. The SSA will automatically adjust these benefits. Once your AIME is calculated, it will then be applied to a formula designed by the SSA to determine your PIA or what you will receive on a monthly basis at FRA. This formula (in the table below) is designed in the spirit of Social Security and will replace a greater percentage of lower wage workers/retirees income than it would a higher wage earner.

2013 Primary Insurance Amount (PIA) Calculation	
AIME	**PIA** (as % of AIME)
$0-791	90%
$791-4,768	$711.90 + 32% of the excess over $791
$4,768+	$1,984.54 + 15% of the excess over $4,768

Source: www.socialsecurity.gov/OACT/COLA/piaformula.html

The average individual benefit payment in 2013 is $1261 per month. For the average married couple both collecting benefits, they are receiving a combined benefit of $2048 per month. Finally, the maximum individual Social Security monthly benefit payable in 2013 is $2533.

It is important to review your individual summary of earnings history with the Social Security Administration (SSA). The summary of your individual earnings can be found on your Social Security statement. Please note that the SSA suspended the annual mailing of the statement to taxpayers in March 2011. The SSA has made the statements available online for all workers, and you can easily print the statement out. Simply go to www.ssa.gov and click on the link "*Get Your Social Security Statement Online*". You will need to register with a username and password as well as verify some information online before you have access which will take you about 5 minutes. You can also go to your local Social Security office to request a Summary Earnings Query (SEQY) (or a Detailed Earnings Query (DEQY) that breaks down earnings and employer names from 1978 to present). Review your earnings record and check it for accuracy. There are millions of W-2s that are either not credited to any taxpayer or recorded to the wrong taxpayer. The SSA will correct any errors or omissions of earnings and provide the proper documentation.

The Social Security Administration no longer mails annual statements. However, everything you need is now easily accessible online at www.ssa.gov and click on the link "Get Your Social Security Statement Online".

In general, your Primary Insurance Amount (PIA) may go down if you take your Social Security benefit before Full Retirement Age (FRA) and your monthly benefit may go up if you take your benefits after FRA. In addition, your spousal/ex-spousal, survivor, disability and child benefit will all be based off your individual PIA. These amounts may be more or less than your individual PIA as we will later learn. You can find your estimated PIA on your Social Security statement or by logging into the retirement estimator on the

SSA website at www.ssa.gov and clicking on the *"Estimate Your Retirement Benefits"* link.

How Long Do You Plan To Live?

George Burns once said: "If you ask what is the single most important key to longevity, I would have to say it is avoiding worry, stress and tension. And if you didn't ask me, I'd still have to say it."

In order to understand the best personal strategies to maximize your total Social Security benefits, it's important to understand today's life expectancy and longevity risk.

Ida May, the first recipient of a monthly Social Security check back in 1940 who went on to live to age 100, was quite an exception back then, but today people are living longer, healthier lifestyles and as a result, are living much longer on average. Life expectancy is of course an unknown since no one can predict exactly how long you will live, yet it is a major factor to consider in helping you maximize your Social Security benefits. So we have to look at some of the averages as well as your personal health and family history. This will give us a much better idea of which strategy makes the most sense for you and your family. The average life expectancy in the United States according to the Society of Actuaries RP-2000 Mortality Tables (see below) is 76.9 years of age, 74.1 for men and 79.5 for women. For a 65 year-old male the average life expectancy is 16.3 more years and for a 65 year-old female the average life expectancy is 19.2 more years. That means half of us on average won't make it past age 83 (using a combined male/female total) and the other half will live beyond age 83 once we make it to age 65. Fortunately or unfortunately, we don't know which half we're in! Now here's where it gets interesting: For those of you that are married, at age 65 there is a 50% chance that one of you will live to age 92 and a 25% chance that one of you will live to age 97! Bottom line is that most of us will have to plan for a 2-person, 3-decade retirement. And of course the longer we live, the more money we will need for us to keep our financial dignity and independence during retirement.

Society of Actuaries RP-2000 Mortality

Single Life Expectancies Based on Annuity 2000 Mortality

The male and female single-life life expectancy tables below are based on the Annuity 2000 mortality table. The Annuity 2000 mortality table was adopted by the National Association of Insurance Commissioners in 1996 as an appropriate table for valuing annuity interests. Most states that require charities to maintain gift annuity reserves now require use of the Annuity 2000 table for computing reserves for recent gifts. The Annuity 2000 table is sex-biased, meaning that males have a different mortality than females. Likewise, the life expectancies derived from the Annuity 2000 table differ between males and females.

Single Life - Male
The life expectancy at each male age is show to its right. For example, the life expectancy of a male age 79 is 10.8 years. This means that there is a 50% chance that a 79 year-old male will live at least another 10.8 years.

Age	Years	Age	Years	Age	Years	Age	Years
5	76.6	33	49.5	61	23.7	89	6.2
6	65.6	34	48.5	62	22.9	90	5.8
7	74.7	35	47.5	63	22.1	91	5.5
8	73.7	36	46.6	64	21.3	92	5.2
9	72.7	37	45.6	65	20.4	93	4.9
10	71.7	38	44.6	66	19.6	94	4.6
11	70.8	39	43.7	67	18.9	95	4.3
12	69.8	40	42.7	68	18.1	96	4.1
13	68.8	41	41.7	69	17.3	97	3.8
14	67.8	42	40.8	70	16.6	98	3.6
15	66.9	43	39.8	71	15.9	99	3.4
16	65.9	44	38.9	72	15.2	100	3.1
17	64.9	45	37.9	73	14.5	101	2.9
18	63.9	46	37	74	13.8	102	2.7
19	63	47	36.1	75	13.2	103	2.4
20	62	48	35.2	76	12.5	104	2.2
21	61	49	34.2	77	11.9	105	2
22	60.1	50	33.3	78	11.3	106	1.8
23	59.1	51	32.4	79	10.8	107	1.6
24	58.1	52	31.5	80	10.2	108	1.4
25	57.2	53	30.7	81	9.7	109	1.3
26	56.2	54	29.8	82	9.2	110	1.1
27	55.2	55	28.9	83	8.7	111	1
28	54.3	56	28	84	8.2	112	0.8
29	53.3	57	27.2	85	7.8	113	0.7
30	52.3	58	26.3	86	7.3	114	0.6
31	51.4	59	25.4	87	6.9	115	0
32	50.4	60	24.6	88	6.5	116	0

Single Life - Female
The life expectancy at each female age is show to its right. For example, the life expectancy of a female age 79 is 12 years. This means that there is a 50% chance that a 79 year-old female will live at least another 12 years.

Age	Years	Age	Years	Age	Years	Age	Years
5	80.7	33	53.1	61	26.5	89	6.5
6	79.7	34	52.1	62	25.6	90	6.1
7	78.7	35	51.2	63	24.8	91	5.7
8	77.7	36	50.2	64	23.9	92	5.4
9	76.7	37	49.2	65	23	93	5.1
10	75.7	38	48.2	66	22.2	94	4.8
11	74.7	39	47.3	67	21.3	95	4.5
12	73.7	40	46.3	68	20.5	96	4.2
13	72.8	41	45.3	69	19.6	97	4
14	71.8	42	44.3	70	18.8	98	3.8
15	70.8	43	43.4	71	18	99	3.5
16	69.8	44	42.4	72	17.2	100	3.3
17	68.8	45	41.4	73	16.4	101	3
18	67.8	46	40.5	74	15.6	102	2.8
19	66.8	47	39.5	75	14.9	103	2.6
20	65.8	48	38.6	76	14.1	104	2.3
21	64.9	49	37.6	77	13.4	105	2.1
22	63.9	50	36.7	78	12.7	106	1.9
23	62.9	51	35.7	79	12	107	1.7
24	61.9	52	34.8	80	11.3	108	1.5
25	60.9	53	33.8	81	10.7	109	1.3
26	60	54	32.9	82	10.1	110	1.2
27	59	55	32	83	9.5	111	1
28	58	56	31.1	84	8.9	112	0.9
29	57	57	30.1	85	8.4	113	0.7
30	56	58	29.2	86	7.9	114	0.6
31	55.1	59	28.3	87	7.4	115	0
32	54.1	60	27.4	88	6.9	116	0

Source: www.pgcalc.com/pdf/singlelife.pdf

Society of Actuaries RP-2000 Mortality

There are two male/female joint and survivor life expectancy tables below.

The tables are based on the Annuity 2000 mortality table. The Annuity 2000 mortality table was adopted by the National Association of Insurance Commissioners in 1996 as an appropriate table for valuing annuity interests. Most states that require charities to maintain gift annuity reserves now require use of the Annuity 2000 table for computing reserves for recent gifts. The Annuity 2000 table is sex-biased, meaning that males have a different mortality than females.

To determine the joint and survivor life expectancy of two people, the younger age male and the older age female, find the two ages, then read the number in the box to the right of the female age. For example, the joint and survivor life expectancy of a couple, male age 62 and female age 62, is 29.9 years. This means that there's a 50% chance that one or the other of them will live at least another 29.9 years.

To view or download entire chart go to: http://www.pgcalc.com/pdf/twolife.pdf

Two Lives, Male and Female, Joint and Survivor, MALE IS THE YOUNGER

Male Age	Female Age	Life Exp.	Male Age	Female Age	Life Exp.	Male Age	Female Age	Life Exp.	Male Age	Female Age	Life Exp.
62	62	29.9	64	64	28	66	66	26.3	68	68	24.4
62	63	29.4	64	65	27.5	66	67	25.7	68	69	23.9
62	64	28.9	64	66	27	66	68	25.2	68	70	23.4
62	65	28.4	64	67	26.5	66	69	24.7	68	71	22.9
62	66	27.9	64	68	26.1	66	70	24.3	68	72	22.5
62	67	27.5	64	69	25.7	66	71	23.9	68	73	22.1
63	63	29	65	65	27.1	67	67	25.3	69	69	23.5
63	64	28.4	65	66	26.6	67	68	24.8	69	70	23
63	65	27.9	65	67	26.1	67	69	24.3	69	71	22.5
63	66	27.5	65	68	25.6	67	70	23.8	69	72	22
63	67	27	65	69	25.2	67	71	23.4	69	73	21.6
63	68	26.6	65	70	24.8	67	72	23	69	74	21.2

FEMALE IS THE YOUNGER											
Female Age	Male Age	Life Exp.	Female Age	Male Age	Life Exp.	Female Age	Male Age	Life Exp.	Female Age	Male Age	Life Exp.
62	62	29.9	64	64	28	66	66	26.2	68	68	24.4
62	63	29.5	64	65	27.7	66	67	25.8	68	69	24
62	64	29.2	64	66	27.3	66	68	25.5	68	70	23.7
62	65	28.9	64	67	27	66	69	25.2	68	71	23.4
62	66	28.6	64	68	26.7	66	70	24.9	68	72	23.1
62	67	28.3	64	69	26.4	66	71	24.6	68	73	22.8
63	63	29	65	65	27.1	67	67	25.3	69	69	23.5
63	64	28.6	65	66	26.8	67	68	24.9	69	70	23.1
63	65	28.3	65	67	26.4	67	69	24.6	69	71	22.8
63	66	27.9	65	68	26.1	67	70	24.3	69	72	22.5
63	67	27.6	65	69	25.8	67	71	24	69	73	22.2
63	68	27.3	65	70	25.5	67	72	23.7	69	74	22

Source: www.pgcalc.com/pdf/twolife.pdf
Copyright © 2005 PG Calc Incorporated

The risk associated with life expectancy, known as longevity risk, is simply the risk of living beyond your life expectancy which of course requires more retirement savings and income to support a longer than expected life. Running out of income in retirement is one of the greatest fears that retirees have today, and living beyond the age you planned to live can turn that fear into reality. Longevity is one of the most important factors we need to consider in order for us to truly maximize our Social Security benefits and collect the greatest amount of benefit during our lifetime. However, longevity is one of the biggest disconnects that we see when we look at Social Security benefits that are currently paying out. In fact, 74% of Americans currently receiving Social Security benefits are receiving reduced amounts. That means they opted to take earlier benefits and get paid less. Taking benefits early may have made sense in the 1930s, but not in today's environment of longer, healthier retirement lifestyles. So why are so many Americans taking the benefit early and permanently reducing their benefits by as much as 25%? Because it's not the Social Security Administration's job to provide advice and show you how to maximize your benefits. They are simply there to show you your benefits and answer your questions.

74% of Americans currently receiving Social Security benefits are receiving reduced amounts.

5   THE INS & OUTS (OF YOUR MONEY)

INCOME, INFLATION, TAXES, AND REDUCTIONS

COLLECTING SOCIAL SECURITY WHILE CONTINUING TO WORK

Working later in life, even after collecting your benefits, can be a way to increase your financial resources, peace of mind, and even your monthly Social Security benefit until you decide to stop working. However, your monthly Social Security benefits and spousal benefits may also be withheld if you make too much income.

The rules in the modern American retirement are changing. As we discussed earlier, the majority of baby boomers entering retirement are not doing so with the security and comfort of a monthly check from a company pension plan and a gold watch for 25 years of service like their parent's or grandparent's generation. Those old defined benefit pension plans for most Americans today have become a thing of the past and have been replaced by defined contribution plans or 401k(s). This means that most Americans in today's modern retirement will have to fund their own retirement and the income will come from individual and employer-sponsored savings. It's no longer as easy as taking the interest and dividends without touching principal in today's environment of low interest rates and high volatility in global stock markets. And of course with long lifespans compared to a generation or two ago, baby boomers have to build diversified retirement portfolios with sustainable withdrawal rates to create a solid retirement income plan.

Another major change in the modern American retirement is a more active lifestyle in retirement. The baby boomers are not a generation that plans to sit on a comfortable rocking chair on their porch. They have much higher expectations of what their retirement will look like compared to their parent's generation. More and more, baby boomers head towards retirement with plans of exotic travel, retirement homes, new cars, spa treatments and 4-star meals— pleasures their parents and grandparents never considered. This newfound active lifestyle of course will require significant savings and income to fund. As a result, more and more baby boomers plan on working during their retirement.

According to a recent study, *The New Retirement Survey*, sponsored by Merrill Lynch and created with guidance from gerontologist and author Ken Dychtwald, Ph.D., 76% of baby boomers intend to keep working and earning in retirement. On average, those surveyed expect to retire from their current career or job at around age 64, but continue to work in an entirely new job, career, or industry. A new career or role they find more rewarding, fulfilling and are passionate about. For most, this isn't going to be a full time role, but a balance between periods of work and leisure. Another factor contributing to baby boomer planning to work beyond traditional retirement age is the concern about the unpredictable cost of healthcare. According to *The New Retirement Survey*, the baby boomer generation is three times more worried about major illness and the associated costs that go with it.

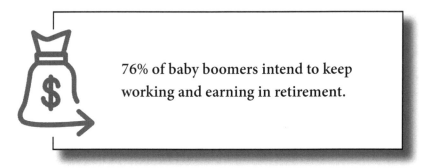

76% of baby boomers intend to keep working and earning in retirement.

Continuing to work in retirement can be a way to increase your financial resources, peace of mind, and even your monthly Social Security benefits until you decide to stop working. However, Social Security has an annual earnings limit that may reduce your monthly Social Security benefits (and perhaps your spousal benefit as well), and in some cases you might not receive any monthly Social Security income at all if you collect it before your Full Retirement Age (FRA). Remember, Social Security was established in part to provide monthly supplemental retirement income, so the Social Security Administration will reduce your monthly benefit if you take your benefits early and continue to work. After you reach your Full Retirement

Age (FRA), the withholding is made up in your benefits.

Here's how it works. The annual earnings limit is a withholding schedule that the Social Security Administration (SSA) has in place that may apply if you continue to work and receive wages and collect your monthly Social Security benefits before reaching Full Retirement Age (FRA). The earnings test only applies to the individual collecting early benefits and does not include earnings or wages from a spouse. However, spousal and family benefits may be withheld as a result of the individual's earnings exceeding the earnings limit thresholds. Earnings for the test are based on income from wages, salary, or self-employment income and must be reported to the SSA. Earnings for the test do not include interest income, withdrawals from retirement plans or investment income like dividends and capital gains. The SSA will reduce or withhold $1 in your monthly Social Security benefit for every $2 you earn above a certain amount if you collect benefits before your FRA. The earnings limit tends to increase every year and for 2013 it was $15,120. In the year in which you turn your FRA, the limit goes up to $40,080. That same year, the SSA withholds $1 in your monthly benefit for every $3 you earn over the $40,080 earnings limit. Once you reach the month you turn your FRA, your earnings and wages no longer affect your monthly Social Security benefit payments.

Here's an example of how it would work. Let's suppose you started taking benefits when you turn 62 in January and you qualify for a monthly Social Security benefit of $1800, or $21,600 annually in benefits. However, you continue to work and earn $43,920 in wages. Using the current earnings limit of $15,120, you are $28,800 over the cap ($43,920 - $15,120 = $28,800). The Social Security Administration (SSA) withholds $1 for every $2 you earn above the limit, which work out to be half of the $28,800 you went over or $14,400. Your total Social Security benefits for the year would only be $7200, not the $21,600 your work history had earned at age 62. $21,600 in earned annual benefits at age 62 - $14,400 in benefits withheld = $7200 in annual benefits received. The SSA will withhold the monthly Social Security benefits until your annual amount withheld is satisfied. In the previous example, $14,400 in earnings was being withheld from you who earned a

$1800 monthly benefit starting at age 62 in January. The SSA would withhold the $1800 monthly benefit from January through August ($1800 per month x 8 months = $14,400). In September you would begin to receive your $1800 monthly Social Security benefit. If your spouse collected a spousal benefit from your earnings history in the above example, both the individual and spousal benefits would be withheld. A monthly earnings test may apply if it provides an individual with better results than the annual test.

Monthly Social Security benefits withheld due to the earnings test are permanently lost. However, your benefits will be adjusted for the months the amounts were withheld at your Full Retirement Age (FRA). The reduction for taking benefits early only apply to the months that you actually receive a monthly Social Security benefit, not the months that were withheld due to the earnings limit test. For example, if your FRA is 66 and you start benefits at age 62, your monthly Social Security benefits are reduced by 25% for early collection. Let's then assume you had one year worth of benefits withheld because you continued to work and earned more in wages than the earnings limit. When you turn your FRA of 66, your monthly Social Security benefits would be adjusted to reflect the one year of benefits withheld and give you credit as if you collected benefits at age 63. Therefore, instead of a 25% reduction in your monthly Social Security benefits for collecting early at age 62, the Social Security Administration would adjust your benefit to a 20% reduction as if you collected at 63. As a reminder, the earnings test does not apply after your FRA. Bottom line, it is important to consider the earnings test if you plan to work past age 62 before collecting your Social Security benefits early.

It is important to consider the earnings test if you plan to work past age 62 before collecting your Social Security benefits early.

In some circumstances, working in retirement after collecting monthly Social Security benefits can actually increase your monthly benefits. Usually, these increases are small, but possible. Every spring, the Social Security Administration recalculates your Primary Insurance Amount (PIA) if the previous year's earnings from working in retirement are higher than one of the 35 years used to calculate your Average Monthly Indexed Earnings (AIME).

COLLECTING SOCIAL SECURITY WITH LITTLE TO NO EARNINGS

This issue can be particularly important for women and stay-at-home moms. If you have not worked or do not have enough Social Security credits, you may still be eligible for Social Security benefits provided you are married, divorced, widowed or caring for a child less than age 16 or disabled. You may be eligible for benefits as early as 62 or earlier if you are widowed or are caring for a disabled child. Additional information for women can be found under the "What Every Woman Should Know" publication on the Social Security Administration website at www.ssa.gov/pubs/10127.html.

INFLATION

Social Security benefits are automatically increased each year to reflect a Cost Of Living Adjustment or COLA. The Cost Of Living Adjustment (COLA) is based on the percentage increase in the Consumer Price Index for Urban Wage Earners and Clerical Earners (CPI-W). The CPI-W is a measure of the average change over time in the prices paid by urban consumers for a basket of consumer goods and services. The CPI-W is determined by the Bureau of Labor Statistics and the Social Security Administration typically makes the announcement for an upcoming COLA between October and December to go in affect the following January. The purpose of a COLA is to ensure that the purchasing power of Social Security benefits is not eroded by the rising costs of goods or services. For example, if the CPI-W is 3% for the year then $1.00 would only buy 97 cents of goods the following year. The $1.00 still has a currency value of $1.00, but it doesn't buy as much "stuff". Over time, inflation can erode a fixed income significantly and reduce the amount of "stuff" money can buy.

Congress enacted the COLA provision in a 1972 amendment and automatic COLA increases began in 1975. The COLA in 2010 and 2011 was 0.0, but in 2012 the COLA was 3.6% and therefore automatically increased Social Security benefit payouts for individuals currently receiving monthly payouts.

A Cost of Living Adjustment (COLA) ensures that the purchasing power of Social Security benefits is not eroded by inflation.

Historical Cost of Living Adjustments (COLAs)			
Automatic Cost Of Living Adjustments			
July 1975	-- 8.0%	January 1995	-- 2.8%
July 1976	-- 6.4%	January 1996	-- 2.6%
July 1977	-- 5.9%	January 1997	-- 2.9%
July 1978	-- 6.5%	January 1998	-- 2.1%
July 1979	-- 9.9%	January 1999	-- 1.3%
July 1980	-- 14.3%	January 2000	-- 2.5%[1]
July 1981	-- 11.2%	January 2001	-- 3.5%
July 1982	-- 7.4%	January 2002	-- 2.6%
January 1984	-- 3.5%	January 2003	-- 1.4%
January 1985	-- 3.5%	January 2004	-- 2.1%
January 1986	-- 3.1%	January 2005	-- 2.7%
January 1987	-- 1.3%	January 2006	-- 4.1%
January 1988	-- 4.2%	January 2007	-- 3.3%
January 1989	-- 4.0%	January 2008	-- 2.3%
January 1990	-- 4.7%	January 2009	-- 5.8%
January 1991	-- 5.4%	January 2010	-- 0.0%
January 1992	-- 3.7%	January 2011	-- 0.0%
January 1993	-- 3.0%	January 2012	-- 3.6%
January 1994	-- 2.6%	January 2013	--1.7%

[1] *The COLA for December 1999 was originally determined as 2.4 percent based on CPIs published by the Bureau of Labor Statistics. Pursuant to Public Law 106-554, however, this COLA is effectively now 2.5 percent.*

Source: www.ssa.gov/cola/automatic-cola.htm

Taxes

A growing number of Americans pay income tax on part of their Social Security benefits. There have been many debates over the years about introducing means testing for Social Security benefits. Means testing, or reducing monthly Social Security benefits to affluent recipients, has been explained as an effective way to reducing the climbing costs of the Social Security program. Means testing would phase out monthly benefits for Americans that make a certain amount of income, say $100,000 for example in retirement. The concept simply stated is that Social Security was created as a means for low and middle-income retirees to help keep their financial dignity and independence in retirement and is not necessary for wealthy Americans. Denying such benefits to the wealthy would make more funds available to continue to help those that need it the most in retirement going forward. The debate over whether to use means testing as a way to fix some of the financial problems the Social Security Administration faces will likely go on for years to come and is not a discussion we are going to engage in. Our goal is to help you make informed decision on how you can maximize your total earned monthly Social Security benefits. However, Social Security already uses a form of means testing and has since 1983 as a result of several amendments that were passed by Congress and signed into law. Effective for taxable years beginning in 1983, Social Security benefits became taxable for the first time for higher income recipients and the additional tax revenues are transferred into the Social Security Trust Fund. Americans with high retirement incomes may pay tax on the majority of the monthly Social Security benefits received. Let's take a closer look.

Most Americans receiving monthly Social Security benefits do not have to pay any federal income tax on their benefits. However, for those retirees who have a substantial income on top of their monthly Social Security benefits, up to 85% of their benefits may be taxable. In addition, there may even be a state or local tax on the benefits so you may want to check with your local tax advisor or state tax authority. Currently, 35 states exempt tax on Social Security benefits. Approximately 35% of Americans that collect monthly Social Security benefits have to pay income taxes on their benefits because their additional income from work, pensions, or investment income exceeds a predetermined limit. See Provisional Income Table below for limits.

> Approximately 35% of Americans pay income taxes on their Social Security benefits because their additional income from work, pensions, or investments exceeds a predetermined limit.

The first step to determine if you may owe income tax on your monthly Social Security benefits is to calculate your "provisional income". Your provisional income is the sum of wages, interest (both taxable and non-taxable-muni bonds, etc.), pension income, dividends, self-employment and other taxable income PLUS 50% of your annual Social Security benefits. Once the provisional income is calculated, the next step is to compare the amount to the IRS thresholds that depend on whether you file as single (head of household) or jointly (married). Up to 85% of your Social Security benefits may be taxable, leaving 15% to remain untaxed for everyone.

The IRS limits depend on your filing status and may be subject to change. Currently, for a single tax payer, provisional income below $25,000 is not taxed. 50% of Social Security benefits may be taxed if provisional income is between $25,000 and $34,000. Up to 85% of Social Security benefits may be taxable if provisional income exceeds $34,000. For joint filers, provisional income below $32,000 is not taxed. 50% of Social Security benefits may be taxed if provisional income is between $32,000 and $44,000. Up to 85% of Social Security benefits may be taxable if provisional income exceeds $44,000. See Provisional Income Table below.

Provisional Income	
Single or Head of Household	**Married Filing Jointly**
Base Amount $25,000 not taxed	Base amount $32,000 not taxed
$25,000-34,000 up to 50% taxable	$32,000-44,000 up to 50% taxable
Above $34,000 up to 85% taxable	Above $44,000 up to 85% taxable

Source: www.socialsecurity.gov/planners/taxes.htm

For example, let's assume you file taxes jointly and your combined annual Social Security benefits (you and your spouse) add up to $24,000. (The Social Security Administration usually sends out an SSA-1099 form every January that tells you your total benefits for the year.) In addition, you receive total taxable pension benefits of $14,000 and interest income of $2000. Your provisional income is $28,000. 50% of $24,000 of Social Security is $12,000 + $14,000 pension income + $2000 interest income = $28,000. Since the combined provisional income of $28,000 does not exceed the $32,000 joint threshold, the Social Security benefits will not be taxed.

Determining exactly how much your Social Security benefits may be taxed can get complicated and is beyond the scope of this publication. It is important to consult with your tax advisor or local tax authority for your personal situation.

OTHER POSSIBLE BENEFIT REDUCTIONS

The Social Security Administration may reduce your benefits, your spousal benefits or survivor benefits if you have spent part of your life working for an employer who wasn't part of the Social Security program. The Windfall Elimination and Government Pension Offset may affect benefits.

If you worked for an employer that was not part of the Social Security program (they did not withhold FICA taxes) the pension you receive from that employer may reduce your individual monthly Social Security benefits. Examples of occupations that may not be part of Social Security include federal, state, or local government agencies, teachers, police officers, firefighters, etc. The Windfall Elimination Provision (WEP) was established in 1983 to reduce the Primary Insurance Amount (PIA) of an individual that is eligible for a pension based on a job that did not contribute FICA taxes.

The Windfall Elimination Provision (WEP) reduces your Primary Insurance Amount (PIA) by affecting the formula that calculates your PIA. As a reminder, your PIA is calculated as follows:

2013 Primary Insurance Amount (PIA) Calculation	
AIME	**PIA** (as % of AIME)
$0-791	90%
$791-4,768	$711.90 + 32% of the excess over $791
$4,768+	$1,984.54 + 15% of the excess over $4,768

Source: www.socialsecurity.gov/OACT/COLA/colaseries.html

Under the Windfall Elimination Provision (WEP), the 90% factor used for the first $791 in Average Indexed Monthly Earnings (AIME) may be reduced up to 40%, unless you have more than 20 years of substantial earnings that paid into the Social Security Trust through FICA payroll taxes. Substantial earnings are defined by the Social Security Administration in the first table below and the reduction factor caused by the WEP for the first $791 in AIME is in the second table:

Amount of Substantial Earnings Each Year for Windfall Elimination Provision (WEP)			
Year	Substantial Earnings	Year	Substantial Earnings
1937-54	$900	1989	$8,925
1955-58	$1,050	1990	$9,525
1959-65	$1,200	1991	$9,900
1966-67	$1,650	1992	$10,350
1968-71	$1,950	1993	$10,725
1972	$2,250	1994	$11,250
1973	$2,700	1995	$11,325
1974	$3,300	1996	$11,625
1975	$3,525	1997	$12,150
1976	$3,825	1998	$12,675
1977	$4,125	1999	$13,425
1978	$4,425	2000	$14,175
1979	$4,725	2001	$14,925
1980	$5,100	2002	$15,750
1981	$5,500	2003	$16,125
1982	$6,075	2004	$16,275
1983	$6,675	2005	$16,725
1984	$7,050	2006	$17,475
1985	$7,425	2007	$18,150
1986	$7,875	2008	$18,975
1987	$8,175	2009-11	$19,800
1988	$8,400	2012	$20,475

Source: www.ssa.gov/pubs/10045.html#a0=3

Windfall Elimination Provision (WEP) % used to calculate Primary Insurance Amount (PIA)	
Years of Substantial Earnings	Percentage
30 or more	90%
29	85%
28	80%
27	75%
26	70%
25	65%
24	60%
23	55%
22	50%
21	45%
20 or less	40%

Source: www.ssa.gov/pubs/10045.html#a0=3

The percentage rises from 45-90% if you have 21-30 years of substantial earnings. If you have 30 or more years of substantial earnings that paid payroll tax into the Social Security Trust, the Windfall Elimination Provision (WEP) is entirely phased out, and there will not be a reduction in the calculation of your Primary Insurance Amount (PIA). Spousal and survivor benefits are not subject to the Windfall Elimination Provision (WEP) calculation. Bottom line, the Windfall Elimination Provision (WEP) may affect individual benefits, but not spousal or survivor benefits.

Windfall Elimination Provision (WEP) may affect individual benefits, but not spousal or survivor benefits.

The Government Pension Offset (GPO) reduces spousal and survivor benefits for individuals that receive a public pension (federal, state or local government positions, firefighters, police department, etc.) and did not pay into the Social Security Trust through FICA payroll taxes. The spousal and/ or survivor monthly Social Security benefits will be reduced by two-third of the spouse/survivor's government pension amount.

Let's go through an example of how the Government Pension Offset (GPO) works. Lets assume that the husband (age 66) takes his monthly Social Security benefit at Full Retirement Age (FRA) and receives $2000 in monthly benefits. His wife (age 66) worked for the state government and did not have any FICA payroll taxes withheld to pay into the Social Security Trust for her entire working years. However, she receives a public pension for her years of service with a monthly benefit of $1800. The husband passes away at age 72 and would usually leave a survivor benefit in the amount of his Primary Insurance Amount (PIA) of $2000. However, because the wife did not pay into the Social Security Trust (i.e. no FICA taxes withheld) and received a monthly public pension benefit of $1800, her survivor benefit is reduced by two-thirds the amount of her monthly pension or $1200 (2/3 x $1800 = $1200). Therefore, the wife's monthly Social Security survivor benefit is $800. $2000 Social Security survivor benefit - $1200 Government Pension Offset = $800 in survivor benefit paid to wife.

Government Pension Offset (GPO) reduces spousal and survivor benefits for individuals that receive a public pension (federal, state or local government positions, firefighters, police department, etc.).

6 Married...

Spousal, Ex-Spousal, and Survivor Benefits

Spousal benefits and survivor benefits are benefits a spouse or widow/er may receive based on his/her other spouse's earnings record, even if that spouse is not eligible for his/her own Social Security benefit based on a lack of work history.

If you are currently married or have been married in the past, you may be entitled to collect Social Security monthly benefits based on your spouse, ex-spouse or deceased spouse's work history. These are two additional benefits that Congress added to the Social Security program back in 1939 to protect retiree's spouses, ex-spouses and widows/ers. The first benefit is a spousal benefit and the second is a survivor benefit. Many Americans don't realize they may be eligible for these types of benefits in addition to their own earned Social Security benefit and as a result are leaving thousands of dollars on the table. And unlike most pension plans, spousal benefits and survivor benefits do not affect or reduce the monthly Social Security benefit of the higher earning spouse or ex-spouse. However, without proper 'joint' retirement income planning before claiming the monthly benefit, one spouse's Social Security decision can have a major impact on the other spouse's monthly payout. Understanding how the spousal and survivor benefits work and are calculated are a very important planning tool on how to maximize and increase your total Social Security benefits for many years to come.

Many Americans don't realize they may be eligible for spousal or survivor benefits in addition to their own Social Security benefit, potentially leaving thousands of dollars on the table.

SPOUSAL/EX-SPOUSAL BENEFITS

So what are spousal benefits and how do they work? There are a few key areas to understanding a spousal benefit. Generally, the lower earning spouse may be eligible for half (50%) of the higher earner's Primary Insurance Amount (PIA) (i.e. the monthly benefit at Full Retirement Age (FRA) or age 66 for most readers). Important to note, there are some limited cases where the higher earning spouse may collect a spousal benefit off the lower earning spouse's record. However, spouses are not allowed to collect a spousal benefit off each other's benefit at the same time. A wife can collect off a husband OR a husband can collect off a wife, but not both at the same time. To keep our understanding of spousal benefits simple and in line with the majority of cases, we will assume the lower earning spouse plans to collect off the higher earning spouse's benefit. The lower earning spouse is entitled to receive the greater of his/her own earned Social Security benefit based on his/her individual earnings record or if eligible, up to 50% of the higher earning spouse's PIA. It is important to note that a spouse will not receive both his/her own earned benefit plus 50% of his/her higher earning spouse's benefit. It is the greater of the two and the difference will be added to the lower earner's own benefit. Said another way, the Social Security Administration will always pay your earned benefit first and add to it any spousal benefit you may be eligible for up to a maximum of 50% of the higher earner's PIA. For example, if the husband's PIA is $1600 per month (higher earning spouse in this example) and the wife's PIA is $500 (lower earning spouse in this example), then the wife will receive the greater of her own earned benefit or 50% of the higher earning spouse's benefit (50% of $1600 = $800). $800 is greater than the $500 benefit the wife earned on her own earnings record. Therefore, the wife will receive her own benefit of $500 plus a spousal benefit of $300 ($800-$500) bringing her total benefits up to $800. Remember, the largest monthly benefit the wife is eligible for is 50% of the husband's benefit, in this case $800. The wife receives an extra $300 spousal benefit added to her own earned benefit of $500, bringing her total monthly benefit up to $800 per month. Simply put, the spousal benefit is the money added to the lower earning spouse's own earned Social Security benefit to bring it up to 50% of the higher earning spouse's PIA.

Calculate the spousal benefit by taking 50% of the higher earner's Primary Insurance Amount and subtracting the lower earner's Primary Insurance Amount.

The lower earning spouse will not receive both his/her own earned benefit plus 50% of the higher earning spouse's benefit. It is the greater of the two and the difference will be added to the lower earner's own benefit.

So now that we understand what a spousal benefit is and how it is calculated, let's examine the question: Who is eligible for a spousal benefit and how you apply for it? Spouses do not need to be eligible for an individual Social Security benefit in order to qualify for a spousal benefit. Eligibility is simply based on whether the current legally married spouse is at least age 62 and has been married for at least one year. In addition, the marriage must be a traditional marriage of one man and one woman. However, the Social Security Administration will recognize common-law marriages in the states that recognize common-law marriage. The one-year marriage rule may be waived under certain circumstances if the spouse is the biological parent of the higher earner's child or if the lower earning spouse was eligible for his/her own earned benefit in the month prior to the marriage.

Spousal benefits are not available to the lower earning spouse until the higher earning spouse either begins collecting his/her own Social Security monthly benefit (as early as age 62) OR the higher earning spouse files for benefits at Full Retirement Age (FRA) and suspends the receipt of the monthly

Social Security benefits for a later date (usually up to age 70). File and Suspend is a strategy in which the spouse is going to file for his/her benefits at FRA, but because he/she doesn't necessarily need or want the income he/she suspends receipt of the actual monthly payment to a future date and the monthly benefit would continue to grow with Delayed Retirement Credits (DRCs) of up to 8% per year until age 70. File and Suspend can only occur at FRA or later.

Spousal benefits are always based off the higher earning spouse's Primary Insurance Amount (PIA), even if the higher earning spouse took his/her monthly Social Security benefit early. In addition, spousal benefits do not receive Delayed Retirement Credits (DRCs) if the higher earning spouse delays receipt of his/her monthly Social Security benefit beyond Full Retirement Age (FRA). For example, let's assume the husband is the higher earning spouse and he has a PIA of $1600 and his FRA is 66. His wife's spousal benefit will always be calculated off his $1600. If the husband take's his benefit early at age 62, his monthly benefit will be reduced to $1200 per month, however his wife's spousal benefit will still be calculated off his $1600 PIA. If the husband waits to age 70 to collect, his monthly benefit will grow to $2112 with his DRCs. However, his wife's spousal benefit will still be calculated off the husband's Primary Insurance Amount of $1600.

> Spousal benefits are always calculated off the higher earning spouse's PIA even if the higher earning spouse took his/her benefit early or delayed collection.

As stated before, spousal benefits are not available to the lower earning spouse until the higher earning spouse either begins collecting his/her own Social Security monthly benefit as early as age 62 OR the higher earning spouse files for benefits at Full Retirement Age (FRA) and suspends the receipt of the monthly Social Security benefits for a later date (usually up to age 70).

The lower earning spouse can collect a spousal benefit as early as age 62 provided the above criteria have been met. However, just like individual benefits, spousal benefits will be reduced if they are taken prior to the lower earning spouse's FRA. See % of Spousal Benefits Received if Collected Early Table below. The monthly reduction for a spousal benefit is 25/36% for each of the first 36 months that benefits are collected before FRA and 5/12% for each month between 37-50 months before FRA. For example, if a lower earning spouse has a FRA of 66 and decides to collect benefits at age 62 and 6 months, the lower earning spouse will receive a reduction of 27.5% on his/her spousal benefit. (25/36% x 36 months) + (5/12% x 6 months) = 27.5%. In addition, if you file for spousal benefits before FRA, you must also file for your individual benefit resulting in a reduced benefit. If filing for benefits at FRA you can choose to file for your own earned individual benefit or a standalone spousal benefit. Collecting a standalone spousal benefit at FRA could allow you to defer receipt of your own earned monthly Social Security benefit and therefore receive Delayed Retirement Credits (DRCs) or bonuses in your monthly benefit up to age 70. It is also important to note that spousal benefits or standalone spousal benefits do not receive DRCs for waiting to collect beyond FRA. Hence, there really isn't a reason to delay receipt of the spousal benefit past FRA. Please refer to the strategy section of this book to maximize your spousal benefit, or visit www.socialsecuritycentral.com and use our proprietary Benefit Maximization Calculator.

Spousal benefits do not receive Delayed Retirement Credits so there is no real benefit to wait beyond Full Retirement Age to collect.

% of Spousal Benefits Received if Collected Early						
Age of Collection						
FRA	62	63	64	65	66	67
65	75%	83.3%	91.7%	100%	--	--
66	70%	75%	83.3%	91.7%	100%	--
67	65%	70%	75%	83.3%	91.7%	100%

Source: www.ssa.gov/oact/quickcalc/earlyretire.html

If a marriage ends, the lower earning spouse may lose eligibility for spousal benefits. However, the divorced lower earning spouse may then be eligible for spousal benefits as an ex-spouse. A divorced spouse can collect a monthly spousal benefit on his/her ex-spouse's earnings record if the lower earning divorced spouse is unmarried, both individuals are at least 62 years old, the marriage lasted at least 10 years and the divorce occurred 2 years or more ago. The two-year wait is waived if the lower earning spouse was eligible for individual benefits at the time of the legal divorce. The spousal benefit rules for the lower earning spouse apply to the lower earning divorced spouse with the exception that the higher earning ex-spouse does not need to file for benefits. However, the higher earning ex-spouse needs to be at least age 62. Finally, if the lower earning divorced spouse remarries, he/she may lose eligibility for the higher earning ex-spouse's spousal benefit, until the new marriage ends. Many divorcees do not realize they may be able to receive an increase in their monthly Social Security benefit by applying for their ex-spouse's spousal benefit. This can really help maximize their Social Security benefit and add thousands of dollars in retirement income. Again, spousal benefits do not affect or reduce the monthly Social Security benefit of the higher earning spouse or ex-spouse.

Many divorcees are unaware that they may be able to collect a spousal benefit from their ex-spouse, potentially leaving thousands of dollars on the table.

SURVIVOR BENEFITS

So now that we covered spousal benefits for both married and divorced couples, let's examine what survivor benefits are and how they work. Survivor benefits are a bit easier to understand than spousal benefits, but there is one key difference to understand: survivor benefits can change depending when the higher earning spouse collected his or her benefit. Therefore, proper 'joint' retirement and Social Security income planning is necessary for couples to consider before claiming a monthly benefit. The higher earning spouse's Social Security decision can have a major impact on the other spouse's monthly payout down the road and can cost the surviving spouse thousands of dollars.

Survivor benefits can change depending when the deceased spouse collected his or her benefit.

A survivor benefit is simply the monthly income that the higher earning spouse is able to pass down to the lower earning surviving spouse (widow or widower). As a side note, there are some limited cases where the higher earning surviving spouse may want to collect the lower earning deceased spouse's survivor benefit. This may occur if the surviving spouse has not yet collected their own earned benefit. Surviving spouses can either collect their own earned benefit OR their survivor benefit from their deceased spouse, but they cannot collect both at the same time. If eligible, the surviving spouse can take one benefit and then switch to another benefit. Surviving spouses do not have to be eligible for their own individual Social Security benefits in order to qualify for a monthly survivor benefit. In order to receive a survivor benefit, the surviving spouse must be at least age 60 and have been legally married to the deceased spouse for at least 9 months before the death occurred. This requirement may be waived if the death was due to military service or an accident OR if the surviving spouse is the parent of the deceased spouse's child and the child is under age 16. If the surviving spouse remarries prior to age 60, he or she may lose eligibility for survivor benefits, unless the remarriage ends. If the surviving spouse remarries after age 60, then eligibility for survivor benefits continue.

> You can collect your own earned benefit or a survivor benefit, but you cannot collect both at the same time.

Surviving spouses may receive up to 100% of the deceased spouse's monthly benefit if that amount is greater than the surviving spouse's own earned monthly Social Security benefit. If the surviving spouse has not yet collected their own individual benefit, they may be eligible to collect a survivor benefit even if the survivor benefit is less than their own benefit and then switch over to their own benefit at a future date. It is important to note that even though the surviving spouse may receive up to 100% of the deceased spouse's monthly benefit, the benefit may still be permanently reduced if the deceased spouse collected his/her monthly Social Security benefit before Full Retirement Age (FRA). Unlike a spousal benefit, which is always calculated off the spouse's Primary Insurance Amount (PIA) (i.e. monthly benefit at Full Retirement Age), survivor benefits may be permanently reduced or permanently higher with Delayed Retirement Credits (DRCs) depending on when the deceased spouse started collecting benefits. For married couples, the decision to take Social Security benefits should be a joint decision because it can permanently affect each other's monthly income and cost thousands of dollars in lost benefits. When we look at whose Social Security benefit women are currently collecting, over two-thirds are collecting all or a portion of their husband's benefit. This further validates the need for more joint planning when making individual Social Security decisions for married couples.

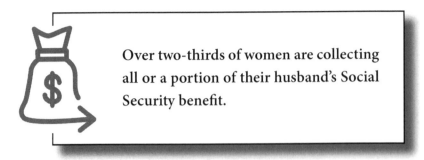

Over two-thirds of women are collecting all or a portion of their husband's Social Security benefit.

In general, if the surviving spouse waits to collect a survivor benefit until his/her own Full Retirement Age (FRA), he/she will be eligible to collect the larger of the deceased spouse's benefit at death or 82.5% of the deceased spouse's Primary Insurance Amount (PIA). See Collecting Survivor Benefits at FRA or Later Table below.

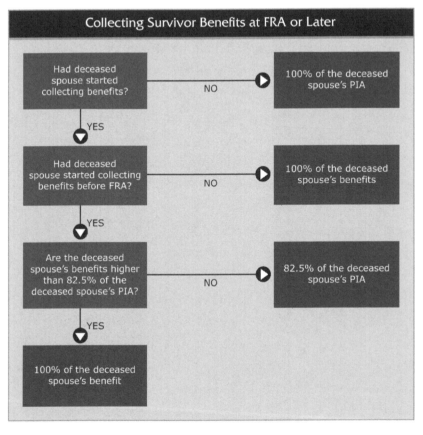

Source: BlackRock's Social Security Benefits:
A Financial Professionals Guide to Fundamental Rules and Collection Strategies

Surviving spouses can receive survivor benefits as early as age 60 (or age 50 if disabled), but monthly survivor benefits will be reduced. If the surviving spouse takes the survivor benefit before his/her FRA, the monthly benefit is reduced for every month the benefit was taken before FRA. The percentage of the monthly reduction is based on the year you were born and what your survivor benefit FRA is. Remember, the FRA for surviving spouses is slightly different than the FRA for individually earned Social Security benefits. On average, the monthly percentage reduction of the survivor benefit is approximately .4%. For example, if your FRA is 66 and you decide to take your survivor benefit at age 64, your benefit will be reduced by approximately 9.6% (.4% monthly reduction x 24 months = 9.6% reduction of monthly benefit). The maximum reduction for a survivor benefit would occur if the surviving spouse decided to take the benefit at age 60. See % of Survivor Benefits Received if Collected Early Table below.

% of Survivor Benefits Received if Collected Early								
	Age of Collection							
FRA	60	61	62	63	64	65	66	67
66	71.5%	76.2%	81%	85.7%	90.5%	95.2%	100%	--
67	71.5%	75.6%	79.6%	83.7%	87.8%	91.9%	95.9%	100%

Source: www.socialsecurity.gov/survivorplan/survivorchartred.htm

In addition, the Collecting Survivor Benefits Before FRA Table below will help determine the survivor benefits to which the surviving spouse/ex-spouse would be entitled.

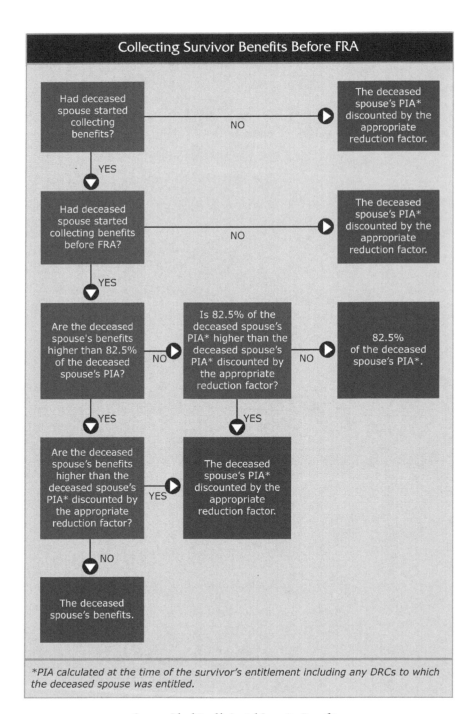

Collecting Survivor Benefits Before FRA

Had deceased spouse started collecting benefits?

— NO → The deceased spouse's PIA* discounted by the appropriate reduction factor.

YES ↓

Had deceased spouse started collecting benefits before FRA?

— NO → The deceased spouse's PIA* discounted by the appropriate reduction factor.

YES ↓

Are the deceased spouse's benefits higher than 82.5% of the deceased spouse's PIA?

NO → Is 82.5% of the deceased spouse's PIA* higher than the deceased spouse's PIA* discounted by the appropriate reduction factor?

NO → 82.5% of the deceased spouse's PIA*.

YES ↓   YES ↓

Are the deceased spouse's benefits higher than the deceased spouse's PIA* discounted by the appropriate reduction factor?

YES → The deceased spouse's PIA* discounted by the appropriate reduction factor.

NO ↓

The deceased spouse's benefits.

*PIA calculated at the time of the survivor's entitlement including any DRCs to which the deceased spouse was entitled.

Source: BlackRock's Social Security Benefits:
A Financial Professionals Guide to Fundamental Rules and Collection Strategies

What if a surviving spouse waits beyond Full Retirement Age (FRA) to collect his/her survivor benefit from his/her deceased spouse? Survivor benefits do not receive Delayed Retirement Credits (DRCs) like an individually earned Social Security benefit would. Therefore, there is no real benefit to wait beyond FRA to collect a survivor benefit. However, a survivor benefit could include the deceased spouse's DRCs. If the surviving spouse takes the survivor benefit at FRA, he/she is entitled to the deceased spouse's Primary Insurance Amount (PIA) including any DRCs the deceased spouse earned. For example, if the deceased spouse had an FRA of 66 and passed away at age 68 but had not yet started his/her monthly Social Security benefit, the surviving spouse would receive the 2 years of DRCs the deceased spouse earned above his/her PIA. This would be a 16% increase (8% increase x 2 years beyond FRA = 16% increase in the PIA).

Survivor benefits do not receive Delayed Retirement Credits so there is no real benefit to wait beyond Full Retirement Age to collect.

So now that you have a better understanding of survivor benefits, here's a quick point to think about when it comes to maximizing your total benefits for a married couple. Let's say you have a husband and wife both age 62. The husband plans to take the benefit as soon as possible at age 62 because he feels it's his money and he's entitled to it. He has paid into the system for 40 some years, and he wants it paid back before he dies or before the system goes broke (his misguided opinion). He wants to start the process as soon as possible. The problem with this mindset is that this decision does not factor in his wife. In other words, the survivor benefit is locked in to the amount when the husband, in this example, takes the money. It's not like a spousal benefit that isn't necessarily going to be locked in. For married couples, the decision to take Social Security benefits should be a joint decision as it can affect each other. The wife has a greater probability of outliving the husband according to the Society of Actuaries RP-2000 Mortality Tables, and she's automatically locked in to a lower amount because the husband took his individual benefit early at age 62. This creates a shortfall of income in terms of what the survivor benefit could have been had it been planned for from the start. It is important to look at maximizing the income and benefit for the person that should live the longest and in this case, it's the wife. The takeaway from this is that most couples look at the decision to take Social Security from a break-even individual perspective. The decision to collect monthly Social Security benefits needs to be a joint life decision, not a single life decision. Refer to the strategy section of this book to maximize your survivor benefit, or visit www.socialsecuritycentral.com and use our proprietary Benefit Maximization Calculator.

In order to maximize a couple's Social Security benefits, the decision of when to claim should be made TOGETHER.

7 ... With Children

Maximizing Benefits Within Your Family

Children's Benefits

More than 4 million children qualify for monthly Social Security benefits as dependents of workers who have retired, died, or become disabled.[2]

Children may be eligible to receive monthly Social Security benefits based off their parent's earnings record. In order to qualify, the parent must file for his/her own earned monthly Social Security retirement benefit or disability benefit. In addition, the child must be under the age of 18 and unmarried OR age 19, unmarried and still in high school. Children 18 or older, but disabled prior to age 22 may also qualify. Children may only collect off one parent's work history but may switch between parents. The monthly Social Security children's benefit will stop once a child turns 18 (or 19 if in high school) or if the disability ends.

Eligible children may receive a monthly payment up to 50% of the parent's Primary Insurance Amount (PIA) or up to 75% of the deceased parent's Primary Insurance Amount (PIA). Benefits paid to children do not decrease the parent's individual benefit. However, there is a limit to the amount paid out to family members. Additional information on Children's Benefits can be found at www.ssa.gov/retire2/yourchildren.htm.

Disability Benefits

More than 16 million Americans receive benefits from at least one of the two Social Security programs designed to pay disability benefits: Social Security Disability Insurance (SSDI) and Supplemental Security Income (SSI).

Over 36 million Americans or approximately 12 percent of the American population are classified as disabled. Half of those disabled Americans are between the working ages of 18 and 64[3]. Even more interesting, according to a Social Security Administration 2011 fact sheet, just over 25% of today's 20 year-olds will become disabled before they retire. Statistically speaking, factors that increase the risk of disability include: excess body weight, tobacco use, high risk activities, occupations, diabetes, high blood pressure, back pain, depression, and frequent alcohol use to name a few. Disability can also strike without warning. One of the fastest growing diseases for Americans age 60 and older is Alzheimer's disease. It is estimated that someone in America develops Alzheimer's every 72 seconds.

Take the case of a baby boomer couple married for 36 years in which both spouses worked. The wife was diagnosed with first-stage Alzheimer's before her 57th birthday and within 9 months she could not hold a job ever again according her neurologist. The couple submitted her disability claim to the Social Security Administration. By her 58th birthday, she received a favorable decision on her claim and began receiving monthly Social Security disability benefits to help offset the loss of income for the couple.

The Social Security disability programs were designed to help with the hardship of having to support yourself or your family if you become disabled and are unable to work. There are two programs administered by the Social Security Administration: Social Security Disability Insurance (SSDI) and Supplemental Security Income (SSI).

Social Security Disability Insurance (SSDI) is a payroll tax funded program managed by the Social Security Administration and is designed to provide monthly benefits to disabled workers and potential family members who depend on them financially. In addition, monthly Social Security disability benefits may go to disabled widows and disabled adult children. There are over 8.3 million disabled Americans receiving Social Security Disability benefits through Social Security Disability Insurance (SSDI)[4].

Disability benefits may be paid out to the disabled wage earner, a spouse who is at least age 62 or caring for the disabled earner's child under age 16,

---

3   U.S. Census Bureau
4   www.ssa.gov

a disabled widow/er who is at least age 50, an unmarried child under age 18 (or 19 if still in high school) or an unmarried child 18 or older who became disabled before age 22.

To qualify for disability benefits, an individual must be so physically or mentally impaired that the individual is not able to perform substantial gainful activity as determined by the Social Security Administration (SSA). To be eligible, the disability must be expected to last for at least 12 months or be a condition that will result in death according to medical evidence. Ultimately, the SSA determines whether these criteria have been met, generally denying two-thirds of filed claims.

Individuals must also have a certain number of work credits from paying FICA payroll taxes to the Social Security Trust. FICA taxes paid by the spouse of the individual applying and FICA taxes paid by the parent of the disabled child applying may count toward the work credits of the individual applying. Some of these credits must be earned in recent years in order to receive disability benefits, unless the disability is blindness. The number of work credits needed depend on the age at which the individual becomes disabled. An individual may qualify with as little a 6 earned credits if the disability occurs before age 24.

Credits Needed to Qualify for Disability Benefits

Unless you are blind, you must have earned at least 20 of the credits in the 10 years immediately before you became disabled.

Born after 1929, Became Disabled at Age	Number of Credits You Need
31 - 42	20
44	22
46	24
48	26
50	28
52	30
54	32
56	34
58	36
60	38
62 or older	40

Source: www.socialsecurity.gov/retire2/credits3.htm

The amount of your monthly Social Security disability benefit depends on your earnings history. The Social Security Administration calculation is very similar to the one used to calculate your individual benefits. In addition, there is a 5-month waiting period before disability benefits begin. Disability benefits cannot be received during these five months; however, disability benefits can be retroactive for up to 12 months. Bottom line, if you believe you qualify for monthly Social Security disability benefits, start the process and apply right away. For more information on disability benefits or to get a rough idea on how much your monthly Social Security disability benefit may be using their calculator, go to www.ssa.gov/dibplan/.

Supplemental Security Income (SSI) is an assistance program for Americans with very little income designed to pay for life's necessities like food, clothing and shelter. SSI is administered by the Social Security Administration (SSA), but is paid for by general tax revenues, not the Social Security Trust. It was created in 1974 and provides benefits to over 8 million Americans.[5] It was created to help Americans with very low incomes and very few financial resources. In order to be eligible to receive monthly SSI benefits, you must be at least 65 years old, blind, or disabled. In addition, you must have income and resources within certain limits. These limits may vary based on the state in which the individual resides as well as the living arrangements and type of income. Financial resources (assets) typically must be below $2000 for a single applicant and $3000 for a couple. If eligible, the monthly Supplemental Security Income (SSI) typically pays up to $710 for an individual and up to $1066 for a couple to help pay for food, clothing or shelter. The SSA has a Benefit Eligibility Screening Tool available at www.ssa.gov/ssi.

Additional Family Benefits

Millions of dependent American family members receive a monthly Social Security check based on the earnings record of a worker's family or auxiliary benefit.

Not only are dependent children and spouses/ex-spouses eligible to receive a monthly benefit, but so are dependent parents. A parent who is over age 62 can receive a monthly Social Security benefit on the record of an adult child. In order to be eligible, the child must have been providing 50% of the financial support to the parent and at the same time, the adult child must have been disabled or passed away. The parent's monthly benefit may terminate if the parent remarries or the parent becomes eligible for his/her own earned monthly Social Security benefit and it exceeds the amount of the parent's benefit.

---

5   www.ssa.gov

There is a provision that sets a cap on the amount of benefits that family members may receive based on the earnings record of one individual: the family maximum. The limit is currently set between 150 and 188 percent of the individual's Primary Insurance Amount (PIA). If the total monthly Social Security benefits going to family members exceed the family maximum, the benefits will be proportionately reduced to bring the total within the limit. The monthly Social Security benefit going to the individual who earned the benefit is not affected or reduced by the family maximum. In addition, benefits payable to an ex-spouse are not included in the family maximum.

PART TWO

Social Security Central LLC Helps Develop YOUR Maximization Strategy

So far, we've looked at the growing role Social Security plays in modern retirement, covered some of the Social Security 'lingo', examined the importance of longevity, and discussed the various benefits available. Let's shift our discussion and examine strategies to maximize your Social Security benefits. Understanding these strategies is key. IT'S YOUR MONEY!

We recognize that every one's situation is unique, and there are many different scenarios that can factor into this discussion. The best strategy for an individual or couple is the one they are most comfortable with. That being said, we are going to cover the most common strategies that help maximize cumulative lifetime Social Security benefits for the majority of eligible individuals.

To get YOUR Social Security maximization strategy in just five minutes, visit www.socialsecuritycentral.com and use our proprietary Benefit Maximization Calculator. IT'S YOUR MONEY!

8 WE'RE ALL IN THIS TOGETHER

10 ASSUMPTIONS THAT APPLY TO ALL STRATEGIES

We are going to make some basic assumptions that apply to all strategies:

- ASSUMPTION #1—For purposes of calculating our income maximization strategies, we will assume Full Retirement Age (FRA) is 66. This will include anyone born between 1945 and 1961. Please see the Full Retirement Age (FRA) Table for your individual FRA. Remember, FRA is the age at which you would receive your full retirement benefit from Social Security. If you take your benefits prior to this age, your benefits and survivor benefits may be reduced. If you take your individual benefits after this age, you may receive more monthly income. Our proprietary Benefit Maximization Calculator can help determine these differences. Age 65 was the original FRA and is gradually being increased to age 67 based on year of birth. The widow/er survivor FRA is slightly different than the individual FRA.

Full Retirement Age (FRA)	
Note: If you qualify for benefits as a survivor (widow/widower) your full retirement age may be different.	
Year of Birth*	**Full Retirement Age**
1937 or earlier	65
1938	65 and 2 months
1939	65 and 4 months
1940	65 and 6 months
1941	65 and 8 months
1942	65 and 10 months
1943-1954	66
1955	66 and 2 months
1956	66 and 4 months
1957	66 and 6 months
1958	66 and 8 months
1959	66 and 10 months
1960 and later	67
*If you were born on January 1st of any year you should refer to the previous year. (If you were born on the 1st of the month, we figure your benefit (and your full retirement age) as if your birthday was in the previous month.)	

- ASSUMPTION #2—Strategies for Singles do not factor in anyone else that may be eligible to receive benefits based on the single individual's earnings record. For example, a child or dependent parent would not be eligible for benefits in these strategies.

- ASSUMPTION #3—Strategies for Couples assume that the couples have been married for at least 1 year. This is the first step in making a spouse eligible to collect spousal benefits. Survivor benefit eligibility is only 9 months, so making the assumption that husband and wife were married for at least 1 year will satisfy eligibility for survivor benefit as well. There are exceptions to the 1-year (or 9-month for survivor) eligibility requirement (e.g. spouse is the parent for the higher wage earner's child), but for purposes of keeping the strategies clear and simple, these exceptions will not factor into these discussions.

- ASSUMPTION #4—Strategies for both Singles and Couples assume that individuals are eligible for Social Security benefits and have satisfied the 40-credit requirement. Remember that an individual pays FICA tax on wages and receives credits for paying this payroll tax. One credit is earned for each $1160 in wages/earnings and an individual can earn a maximum of 4 credits per year. Once an individual acquires 40 credits (approximately 10 years) he/she is eligible to receive Social Security monthly benefits and is considered fully insured. It is also important to note that being eligible or fully insured does not mean that you will receive the maximum Social Security benefit. Once you are eligible, your payout is determined by your Average Indexed Monthly Earnings (AIME) and the age you begin to collect monthly benefits.

- ASSUMPTION #5—Social Security benefits can be collected at any time between ages 62 and 70. To keep thing simple, we examine 3 different ages to collect benefits: age 62, Full Retirement Age (FRA) or age 66 (as assumed in these strategies), and age 70.

- ASSUMPTION #6—The Society Of Actuaries RP-2000 Mortality Tables are used to calculate life expectancies. Ages are rounded; for example, age 87.6 would be rounded up to age 88. A single male age 62 has a life expectancy of 85. In other words, there is a 50% chance that a 62 year-old male will live another 23 years to age 85. The following life expectancies are used:

Single Male		Single Female	
Age	Lives to	Age	Lives to
62	85	62	88
66	86	66	88
70	86	70	88

Married (Joint) Couple	
Age of Both Spouses	One of the Spouses Lives to
62	92

- ASSUMPTION #7— The following Social Security Administration (SSA) tables are used in calculating the percentage of benefits received if collected prior to Full Retirement Age (FRA):

% Individual Benefits Received if Collected Early						
	Age of Collection					
FRA	62	63	64	65	66	67
65	80%	86.7%	93.3%	100%	--	--
66	75%	80%	86.7%	93.3%	100%	--
67	70%	75%	80%	86.7%	93.3%	100%

% of Spousal Benefits Received if Collected Early						
Age of Collection						
FRA	**62**	**63**	**64**	**65**	**66**	**67**
65	75%	83.3%	91.7%	100%	--	--
66	70%	75%	83.3%	91.7%	100%	--
67	65%	70%	75%	83.3%	91.7%	100%

% of Survivor Benefits Received if Collected Early								
Age of Collection								
FRA	**60**	**61**	**62**	**63**	**64**	**65**	**66**	**67**
66	71.5%	76.2%	81%	85.7%	90.5%	95.2%	100%	--
67	71.5%	75.6%	79.6%	83.7%	87.8%	91.9%	95.9%	100%

- ASSUMPTION #8—SSC is the acronym for Social Security Central LLC.

- ASSUMPTION #9—There are many factors that can change these claiming strategies and lifetime cumulative income amounts. For a customized strategy built around your personal circumstances it is recommended that you visit our quick and simple to use Benefit Maximization Calculator at www.socialsecuritycentral.com and/or talk to your financial professional.

- ASSUMPTION #10—Finally, it is important to note that these strategies are based on current promises made by the Social Security Administration at the time of publication. Changes to the law can and will affect these strategies going forward.

If you are single (never-married) the most important factor to maximize your Social Security benefit is your life expectancy. As we have stated before, your monthly Social Security benefit amount will depend on the age you decide to start collecting benefits. For example, if your Primary Insurance Amount (PIA) at your Full Retirement Age (FRA) of 66 is $2000 per month, collecting the benefit early at age 62 would decrease it to $1500 per month (75% x $2000) and waiting to collect the benefit until age 70 would increase the benefit to $2640 (132% x $2000). The Social Security Administration's actuaries calculate the factors that reduce or increase the monthly benefits to be actuarially consistent. What this means is, if you live to age 80 (the average combined life expectancy between men and women), the cumulative benefits received up to age 80 will be approximately the same regardless of when you began collecting benefits. For example, using the numbers in the example above ($1500 per month at age 62, $2000 at age 66 and $2640 at age 70) your cumulative benefits collected up to age 80 are as follows:

Cumulative Lifetime Benefits Through Age 80		
Collect at age 62	Collect at age 66 (FRA)	Collect at age 70
$324,000	$336,000	$316,800

As you can see, these options are all approximately the same cumulative dollar amount, with collecting at age 66 (FRA) providing you slightly more. However, the amounts will change considerably based on your individual life expectancy. Let's assume, that you are not in good health and your life expectancy is only 72. Based on this lower life expectancy, collecting your Social Security benefits at age 62 would maximize your cumulative benefits:

Cumulative Lifetime Benefits Through Age 72		
Collect at age 62	Collect at age 66 (FRA)	Collect at age 70
$180,000	$144,000	$63,360

Let's assume, that you are in good health and have longevity in your family history. Perhaps one of your parents is still alive at age 95. Let's assume that you expect to live a long life as well, and we change your life expectancy to age 95. Based on this longer life expectancy, collecting your Social Security benefits at age 70 would maximize your cumulative benefits:

Cumulative Lifetime Benefits Through Age 95		
Collect at age 62	Collect at age 66 (FRA)	Collect at age 70
$594,000	$696,000	$792,000

As you can see, collecting your benefits early at age 62, but having a longer than average life expectancy can cost you hundreds of thousands of dollars. In this example, it would have cost you $198,000!

If you are single and never-married, the most important factor to maximize your Social Security benefit is your life expectancy.

Finally, let's look at what the RP-2000 Mortality Table calculates our average life expectancy to be based on gender and current age:

Single Male		Single Female	
Age	Lives to	Age	Lives to
62	85	62	88

Cumulative Lifetime Benefits Through Age 85 (Male)		
Collect at age 62	Collect at age 66 (FRA)	Collect at age 70
$414,000	$456,000	$475,200

Cumulative Lifetime Benefits Through Age 88 (Female)		
Collect at age 62	Collect at age 66 (FRA)	Collect at age 70
$468,000	$528,000	$570,240

So let's summarize the best strategy to maximize benefits for a single individual. If your life expectancy is less than age 80, you are better off collecting benefits early at age 62. If your life expectancy is right around age 80, then you are best taking benefits at Full Retirement Age (FRA) or age 66 (as assumed in these strategies). See the Full Retirement Age (FRA) Table for your FRA based on the year you were born. If your life expectancy is well beyond age 80, then you should delay taking benefits up to age 70.

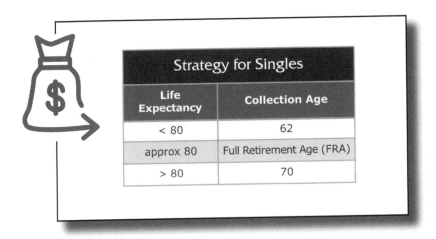

Strategy for Singles	
Life Expectancy	**Collection Age**
< 80	62
approx 80	Full Retirement Age (FRA)
> 80	70

These examples compare different ages at which you collect Social Security benefits and their cumulative totals. This is the easiest way to understand how to maximize your Social Security benefits. We call this the cumulative lifetime benefit approach. There are a few other factors that could change the decision when you decide to begin collecting your Social Security benefits. A present value calculation may be another method to calculate a claiming strategy. This is more complicated than the scope of Social Security Central LLC's goal of keeping your Social Security maximization strategy simple. In a low interest rate environment (like that of 2012 when this book was written), the present value calculation approach won't change the outcome much, if any, from the cumulative lifetime benefit approach.

To get YOUR Social Security maximization strategy in just five minutes, visit www.socialsecuritycentral.com and use our proprietary Benefit Maximization Calculator. IT'S YOUR MONEY!

10 DEFINING YOU

STRATEGIES FOR MARRIED COUPLES

For married couples, life expectancies for each spouse will factor in similar to a single individual; however, spousal benefits and survivor benefits, along with switching between or adding benefits will also play a role in maximizing the total cumulative Social Security benefits. In addition, the difference between each spouse's individual earned benefit will help determine the best strategy to maximize benefits. There are many different scenarios that could affect the timing of claiming your Social Security benefits: different ages, working, not working, life expectancy, etc. In the scope of our discussion, we will examine the three most common strategies that occur amongst couples similar in age and use average joint life expectancy for a 62 year-old couple from the RP-2000 Mortality Tables. These tables assume that for a 62 year-old couple there is a 50% chance that one of the spouses will live to age 92. Finally, we will use a fictitious married couple, Tom and Cindy both age 62, to make the following strategies simple and easy to follow. We will look at the cumulative lifetime Social Security benefits for Tom and Cindy if they claim benefits at age 62, Full Retirement Age (FRA) 66, and 70.

OPTION A—
MARRIED w/BIG DIFFERENCE IN EARNED BENEFITS

PROPOSED SSC STRATEGY =
Collect Now File And Suspend (CNFAS)

This strategy is designed for a couple where one of the spouse's own earned benefit is significantly greater than the other spouse's earned benefit. The benefits have a large enough difference in value that the Primary Insurance

Amount (PIA) of the lower earning spouse is less than the spousal benefit. In other words, **the lower earning spouse's PIA is less than 50% of the higher earning spouse's PIA.**

Tom and his wife Cindy are both age 62. Tom had a successful career and Cindy left the workforce for a period of time to raise their children. As a result, Tom is the higher earning spouse and has a Primary Insurance Amount (PIA) at Full Retirement Age (FRA) 66 of $2000. Cindy's PIA at FRA 66 is $700. Let's assume that Tom lives to age 80 (passes away the month he turns 80) and Cindy lives to age 92 (passes away the month she turns 92). Remember, for a 62 year-old couple there is a 50% chance that one of the two spouses will live to age 92. If Tom collects his benefit before his FRA at age 62, his monthly benefit is reduced to $1500. 75% of Tom's PIA of $2000 = $1500. In addition, since Tom collected his benefit early, he has permanently reduced Cindy's survivor benefit when Tom passes away to 82.5% of Tom's PIA of $2000 or $1650 per month. If Tom collects his benefit at FRA 66 he will receive his $2000 monthly benefit and Cindy's survivor benefit when Tom passes away will also be $2000. Finally, if Tom waits to collect his benefit at age 70, he will receive $2640 per month until he passes away and Cindy's survivor benefit will also be $2640. The Delayed Retirement Credits (DRCs) increase Tom's PIA of $2000 by 8% each year until he turns 70, a total increase of 32% ($2000 x 132% = $2640).

Cindy can collect her benefit at age 62 and receive $525 per month. By collecting early, Cindy's PIA of $700 is reduced. 75% of Cindy's PIA of $700 = $525. If Tom has already filed for his benefits, Cindy is also able to collect a spousal benefit of $210 on top of her $525. Cindy's reduced earned benefit of $525 + reduced spousal benefit of $210 = $735. The spousal benefit is calculated by taking 50% of the higher earner's PIA and subtracting the lower earner's PIA. This amount is then added to the lower earner's monthly benefit. Because Cindy is collecting the spousal benefit before her FRA of 66, it is reduced. Tom's PIA of $2000 x 50% ($1000) – Cindy's PIA of $700 = $300 in spousal benefit. The $300 spousal benefit is reduced by 30% (to $210) because Cindy collected it early at age 62. If Cindy waits until her

Full Retirement Age (FRA) of 66 to collect her own benefit, she will receive her Primary Insurance Amount (PIA) of $700. In addition, she will be able to collect a spousal benefit of $300 for a total of $1000 in benefits. Cindy's earned benefit of $700 + spousal benefit of $300 = $1000. If she waits to collect her earned benefit until age 70, her monthly benefit will increase by 32% because of Delayed Retirement Credits (DRCs) to $924 per month ($700 x 132% = $924). In addition, she will be able to collect a spousal benefit of $76 for a total of $1000 in benefits. Cindy's earned benefit of $924 + spousal benefit of $76 = $1000. Keep in mind that spousal benefits do not receive Delayed Retirement Credits. The spousal benefit remains to be 50% of Tom's PIA of $2000 or $1000.

Because Tom is the higher earning spouse, his earned benefits will continue not just until he passes away at age 80, but will also provide Cindy's survivor benefit until she passes away at age 92. This is an important point to remember because claiming Social Security benefits for a couple is not an individual decision, but a joint decision and should examine each spouse's life expectancy. **In general, the age at which the higher earning spouse should claim his/her Social Security benefit is based on the life expectancy of the lower earning spouse. And the age at which the lower earning spouse should claim his/her benefit is based on the life expectancy of the higher earning spouse.** The higher earning spouse Tom should claim his benefit based on his wife Cindy's life expectancy since his survivor benefit will continue after his death and provide Cindy with a higher income for her remaining years. In addition, the lower income earning spouse Cindy should claim her benefit based on the higher income earning spouse Tom's life expectancy. For a married couple with a big difference in earned monthly Social Security benefits such as Tom and Cindy, Tom should claim his benefit based on Cindy's life expectancy of 92 and therefore take his Social Security benefit at age 70, even though he passes away at 80. Cindy should take her benefit at age 62 based on Tom's shorter life expectancy of age 80. If Tom had a longer than normal life expectancy and lived well into his 90s and beyond, a different strategy may be appropriate including

Cindy claiming her individual and spousal benefit at a later time. So, now that we understand the relationship of life expectancy for a couple with a big difference in earned monthly Social Security benefits, we present the Collect Now File And Suspend (CNFAS) strategy.

In general, the age at which the higher earning spouse should claim his/her Social Security benefit is based on the life expectancy of the lower earning spouse. And the age at which the lower earning spouse should claim his/her benefit is based on the life expectancy of the higher earning spouse.

Here's how it works: Cindy, the lower earning spouse, collects her benefits at age 62 before her Full Retirement Age (FRA) and receives a reduced benefit of $525 per month and Tom does nothing. Cindy's Primary Insurance Amount (PIA) is $700, but she only receives 75% of this amount, or $525, because she collects early at age 62. When Tom turns 66, his FRA, he files for and suspends his monthly benefit. By filing and suspending, Cindy is now able to collect Tom's spousal benefit. Remember, the spousal benefit is calculated by taking 50% of the higher earner's Primary Insurance Amount (PIA) and subtracting the lower earner's PIA. This amount is then added to the lower earner's monthly benefit. In the case of Tom and Cindy the spousal benefit is $300 per month. 50% of Tom's $2000 PIA ($1000) – Cindy's PIA of $700 = $300. Cindy's spousal benefit is not reduced as she is taking it at her FRA of 66. Adding $300 per month to Cindy's already $525 monthly benefit would provide Cindy with total benefits of $825 per month. Since Tom suspends his monthly benefit, he will receive Delayed Retirement Credits (DRCs) until age 70. At age 70, Tom collects his maximum benefit of $2640 ($2000 x 132%). When Tom passes away at age 80, Cindy will then receive a survivor benefit of $2640 for the rest of her life, which in this case is another 12 years! (Cindy's survivor benefit is the larger of her earned benefit or Tom's earned benefit based on his record.)

Let's look at the cumulative benefits for claiming at ages 62, 66 (FRA), 70 and then examine the strategy that maximizes the total cumulative Social Security benefits for a married couple with a big difference in monthly earned Social Security benefits:

Monthly Benefits											
	Collect at 62			Collect at 66			Collect at 70			Collect CNFAS		
Ages	Tom	Cindy	Spousal	Tom	Cindy	Spousal	Tom	Cindy	Spousal	Tom	Cindy	Spousal
62/62	$1500	525	210*							$0	525	
63/63	$1500	525	210							$0	525	
64/64	$1500	525	210							$0	525	
65/65	$1500	525	210							$0	525	
66/66	$1500	525	210	$2000	700	300				$0	525	300
67/67	$1500	525	210	$2000	700	300				$0	525	300
68/68	$1500	525	210	$2000	700	300				$0	525	300
69/69	$1500	525	210	$2000	700	300				$0	525	300
70/70	$1500	525	210	$2000	700	300	$2640	924	76	$2640	525	300
71/71	$1500	525	210	$2000	700	300	$2640	924	76	$2640	525	300
72/72	$1500	525	210	$2000	700	300	$2640	924	76	$2640	525	300
73/73	$1500	525	210	$2000	700	300	$2640	924	76	$2640	525	300
74/74	$1500	525	210	$2000	700	300	$2640	924	76	$2640	525	300
75/75	$1500	525	210	$2000	700	300	$2640	924	76	$2640	525	300
76/76	$1500	525	210	$2000	700	300	$2640	924	76	$2640	525	300
77/77	$1500	525	210	$2000	700	300	$2640	924	76	$2640	525	300
78/78	$1500	525	210	$2000	700	300	$2640	924	76	$2640	525	300
79/79	$1500	525	210	$2000	700	300	$2640	924	76	$2640	525	300
80/80	$0	1650	0	$0	2000	0	$0	2640		$0	2640	0
/81	$0	1650	0	$0	2000	0	$0	2640		$0	2640	0
/82	$0	1650	0	$0	2000	0	$0	2640		$0	2640	0
--	--	--	--	--	--	--	--	--	--	--	--	--
/91	$0	1650	0	$0	2000	0	$0	2640		$0	2640	0
/92	$0	0	0	$0	0	0	$0	0		$0	0	0
Cumulative Combined Lifetime Benefits											
$720,360				$792,000			$816,960			$860,760		

*The spousal benefit is reduced because it was collected early. If your Full Retirement Age (FRA) is 66 and you collect spousal benefits at age 62, the benefit is reduced by 30%. Tom's Primary Insurance Amount of $2000 x 50% – Cindy's Primary Insurance Amount of $700 = $300 in spousal benefit. The $300 spousal benefit is reduced by 30% or $90. $300 - $90 = $210.

As you can see, the Collect Now File And Suspend (CNFAS) strategy generated the greatest amount of cumulative lifetime Social Security benefits for Tom and Cindy. **If Tom and Cindy simply took their benefits each at age 62 without thinking about or knowing how to maximize their benefits, they would have lost out on $140,400 in cumulative lifetime Social Security benefits that they worked hard for and earned!**

In our example, Tom and Cindy are both the same age. If the lower earning spouse Cindy was younger, it becomes even more important for Tom to delay his benefits past Full Retirement Age (FRA) because Tom's survivor benefit pays Cindy for even longer. If Cindy were 5 years younger than Tom, but still lives to age 92 and Tom passes away at the same age of 80, then Cindy would receive Tom's survivor benefit for 17 years! Even if Tom (the higher earning spouse) was 5 years younger than Cindy (the lower earning spouse), it still makes sense for Tom to delay collecting his Social Security benefits until age 70. The Collect Now File And Suspend (CNFAS) strategy still may make sense, but the difference is not as great. This is because Tom's survivor benefit doesn't pay Cindy for as long. When Tom passes away at age 80, Cindy is already 85 years old. She will collect Tom's survivor benefit for 7 more years until her passing at age 92.

OPTION B—
MARRIED W/SMALL DIFFERENCE IN EARNED BENEFITS

PROPOSED SSC STRATEGY =
File And Suspend Collect Later (FASCL)

This strategy is designed for a couple that has similar earned benefits. The benefits are close enough in value that the Primary Insurance Amount (PIA) of the lower earning spouse is typically greater than the spousal benefit. In other words, **the lower earning spouse's PIA is typically greater than 50% of the higher earning spouse's PIA.**

Tom and his wife Cindy both are age 62. Both Tom and Cindy had very successful careers and are at the point in their lives where they want to trade in their corporate jobs and do something different. They are both high-income earners. Tom has a Primary Insurance Amount (PIA) at Full Retirement Age (FRA) 66 of $2000. Cindy's PIA at FRA 66 is $1600. Let's assume that Tom lives to age 80 (passes away the month he turns 80) and Cindy lives to age 92 (passes away the month she turns 92). Remember, for a 62 year-old couple there is a 50% chance that one of the two spouses will live to age 92. If Tom collects his benefit at age 62, which is before his FRA of 66, his monthly benefit is reduced to $1500. 75% of Tom's PIA of $2000 = $1500. In addition, since Tom collected his benefit early, he has permanently reduced Cindy's survivor benefit when Tom passes away to 82.5% of Tom's PIA of $2000 or $1650 per month. If Tom collects his benefit at FRA 66 he will receive his $2000 monthly benefit and Cindy's survivor benefit when Tom passes away will also be $2000. Finally, if Tom waits to collect his benefit at age 70, he will receive $2640 per month until he passes away and Cindy's survivor benefit will also be $2640. The Delayed Retirement Credits (DRCs) increase Tom's PIA of $2000 by 8% each year until he turns 70, a total increase of 32% ($2000 x 132% = $2640).

Cindy can collect her benefit early at age 62 and receive $1200 per month. Because Cindy collects at age 62 and not her Full Retirement Age (FRA) of 66, her Primary Insurance Amount (PIA) of $1600 is reduced. 75% of Cindy's PIA of $1600 = $1200. Also, Cindy is not able to collect a spousal benefit at age 62, even though Tom filed for his own earned benefit at 62. Why not? Because if she applies for spousal benefits before reaching FRA 66, the Social Security Administration requires her to apply for both her own earned benefit as well as the spousal benefit, and because her own earned benefit is greater than the spousal benefit, she will receive the greater of the two amounts, but not both. The spousal benefit is calculated by taking 50% of the higher earner's PIA and then subtracting the lower earner's PIA. 50% of Tom's PIA of $2000 = $1000. Cindy's own earned PIA is $1600 and is greater than 50% of Tom's PIA of $1000. Therefore, Cindy will not receive a spousal benefit. If Cindy waits to her FRA of 66 to collect her own benefit, she will receive her PIA of $1600. Again, Cindy will not receive a spousal benefit because her own earned benefit of $1600 is greater than the spousal benefit at FRA. Cindy's own earned PIA is $1600 and is greater than 50% of Tom's PIA (50% x $2000 = $1000). If Cindy waits to collect her earned benefit until age 70, her monthly benefit will increase by 32% because of Delayed Retirement Credits (DRCs) to $2112 per month ($1600 x 132% = $2112). Once again, there would be no spousal benefit because 50% of Tom's PIA is less than Cindy's PIA (50% of $2000 = $1000. $1000 is less than $1600).

Since Tom is the higher earning spouse, his earned benefits will continue not just until he passes away at age 80, but will also provide Cindy's survivor benefit until she passes away at age 92. This is an important point to remember because claiming Social Security benefits for a couple is not an individual decision, but a joint decision and should examine each spouse's life expectancy. **In general, the age at which the higher earning spouse should claim his/her Social Security benefit is based on the life expectancy of the lower earning spouse. And the age at which the lower earning spouse should claim his/her benefit is based on the life expectancy of the higher earning spouse.** The higher earning spouse Tom should claim his benefit based on his wife Cindy's life expectancy since his survivor benefit will continue after his death and provide Cindy with a higher income for her remainder years. For a married couple with a small difference in earned monthly Social Security benefits such as Tom and Cindy, Tom should claim his benefit based on Cindy's life expectancy of 92 and therefore take his Social Security benefit at age 70, even though he passes away at 80. Now that we understand the relationship of life expectancy for a couple with a small difference in earned monthly Social Security benefits, we present the File And Suspend Collect Later (FASCL) strategy.

Here's how it works: Tom, the slightly higher earning spouse, files for and suspends his Social Security benefit at his Full Retirement Age (FRA) of 66. Cindy, the slightly lower earning spouse, collects the spousal benefit at her FRA of 66. In our example, this amount is $1000. 50% of Tom's PIA of $2000 = $1000. It is important to note that she did not collect her own earned benefit, but is simply collecting her spousal benefit based off Tom filing for his benefit but suspending collection. At FRA and beyond, you have the choice of collecting your own earned benefit, collecting a spousal benefit only or collecting both if eligible. By collecting a spousal benefit only, Cindy's own earned benefit can receive Delayed Retirement Credits (DRCs) until she turns age 70. Her benefit at age 70 is worth $2112. Cindy's PIA of $1600 at age 66 receives an 8% increase each year up to age 70 or a 32% total increase. $1600 x 132% = $2112. In addition, since Tom filed for, but suspended his own earned benefit, his benefit will also receive DRCs up until age 70. His own earned benefit at age 70 is worth $2640. Tom's PIA of $2000 x 132% = $2640. When Tom passes away at age 80, Cindy will then receive a survivor benefit of $2640 for the rest of her life, which in this case is another 12 years! (Cindy's survivor benefit is the larger of her earned benefit or Tom's earned benefit based on his record.)

Let's look at the cumulative benefits for claiming at ages 62, 66 (FRA), 70 and then examine the strategy that maximizes the total cumulative Social Security benefits for a married couple with a small difference in monthly earned Social Security benefits:

Monthly Benefits

Ages	Collect at 62 Tom	Cindy	Collect at 66 Tom	Cindy	Collect at 70 Tom	Cindy	Collect CNFAS Tom	Cindy	Spousal	Collect FASCL Tom	Cindy	Spousal
62/62	$1500	1200					$0	1200				
63/63	$1500	1200					$0	1200				
64/64	$1500	1200					$0	1200				
65/65	$1500	1200					$0	1200				
66/66	$1500	1200	$2000	1600			$0	1200	0	$0	0	1000
67/67	$1500	1200	$2000	1600			$0	1200	0	$0	0	1000
68/68	$1500	1200	$2000	1600			$0	1200	0	$0	0	1000
69/69	$1500	1200	$2000	1600			$0	1200	0	$0	0	1000
70/70	$1500	1200	$2000	1600	$2640	2112	$2640	1200	0	$2640	2112	0
71/71	$1500	1200	$2000	1600	$2640	2112	$2640	1200	0	$2640	2112	0
72/72	$1500	1200	$2000	1600	$2640	2112	$2640	1200	0	$2640	2112	0
73/73	$1500	1200	$2000	1600	$2640	2112	$2640	1200	0	$2640	2112	0
74/74	$1500	1200	$2000	1600	$2640	2112	$2640	1200	0	$2640	2112	0
75/75	$1500	1200	$2000	1600	$2640	2112	$2640	1200	0	$2640	2112	0
76/76	$1500	1200	$2000	1600	$2640	2112	$2640	1200	0	$2640	2112	0
77/77	$1500	1200	$2000	1600	$2640	2112	$2640	1200	0	$2640	2112	0
78/78	$1500	1200	$2000	1600	$2640	2112	$2640	1200	0	$2640	2112	0
79/79	$1500	1200	$2000	1600	$2640	2112	$2640	1200	0	$2640	2112	0
80/80	$0	1650	$0	2000	$0	2640	$0	2640	0	$0	2640	0
/81	$0	1650	$0	2000	$0	2640	$0	2640	0	$0	2640	0
/82	$0	1650	$0	2000	$0	2640	$0	2640	0	$0	2640	0
--	--	--	--	--	--	--	--	--	--	--	--	--
/91	$0	1650	$0	2000	$0	2640	$0	2640	0	$0	2640	0
/92	$0	0	$0	0	$0	0	$0	0	0	$0	0	0

Cumulative Combined Lifetime Benefits

$820,800	$892,800	$950,400	$956,160	$998,400

As you can see, the File And Suspend Collect Later (FASCL) strategy generated the greatest amount of cumulative lifetime Social Security benefits for Tom and Cindy. **If Tom and Cindy simply took their benefits each at age 62 without thinking about or knowing how to maximize their benefits, they would have lost out on $177,600 in cumulative lifetime Social Security benefits that they worked hard for and earned!**

In our example, Tom and Cindy are both the same age. For a married couple with a small difference in monthly earned Social Security benefits where the spouses are different ages, the maximization strategies become more complicated. If the lower earning spouse Cindy was younger, it becomes even more important for Tom to delay his benefits past Full Retirement Age (FRA). However, the File And Suspend Collect Later (FASCL) strategy may not generate the most cumulative lifetime income compared to other strategies. If Cindy is 5 years younger than Tom, Cindy should collect her own earned benefit at age 62 which would allow Tom to collect a spousal benefit at age 67. Tom is 5 years older than Cindy and cannot receive a spousal benefit until Cindy collects her benefit. Since Tom is collecting a spousal only benefit, his own earned benefit will continue to receive Delayed Retirement Credits (DRCs) until he turns age 70. At age 70 he collects his earned benefit of $2640 until he passes away at age 80. Cindy would then receive Tom's survivor benefit of $2640 for 17 years! If Tom (the slightly higher earning spouse) was 5 years younger than Cindy (the slightly lower earning spouse), the File And Suspend Collect Later (FASCL) strategy will again make the most sense, but with a slight variation. Cindy, the older spouse, should file for and suspend her benefit until age 70. However, since Tom is younger than Cindy, he will be the one that collects the spousal only benefit at his FRA of 66. He should then switch to his own individual benefit at age 70, which is worth $2640 due to Delayed Retirement Credits. When Tom passes away at age 80, Cindy will then receive a survivor benefit of $2640 for the rest of her life, which in this case is another 7 years! (Cindy's survivor benefit is the larger of her earned benefit or Tom's earned benefit based on his record.)

OPTION C—
MARRIED W/SMALL DIFFERENCE IN EARNED BENEFITS AND SHORTER LIFE EXPECTANCY

PROPOSED SSC STRATEGY =
Collect Now Collect Later (CNCL)

This strategy sets up to be very similar to the previously mentioned Option B File And Suspend Collect Later (FASCL) strategy. The benefits are close enough in value that the Primary Insurance Amount (PIA) of the lower earning spouse is typically greater than the spousal benefit. In other words, **the lower earning spouse's PIA is typically greater than 50% of the higher earning spouse's PIA.** *However, the key difference in this strategy is that the higher earning spouse has a shorter than average life expectancy.*

Tom and his wife Cindy both are age 62. Both Tom and Cindy had very successful careers; however, Tom's health is deteriorating so they want to trade in their corporate jobs and make the most of their remaining years together. Tom has a Primary Insurance Amount (PIA) at Full Retirement Age (FRA) 66 of $2000. Cindy's PIA at FRA 66 is $1600. Let's assume that Tom lives to age 72 (passes away the month he turns 72) and Cindy lives to age 92 (passes away the month she turns 92). Remember, for a 62 year-old couple there is a 50% chance that one of the two spouses will live to age 92. If Tom collects his benefit at age 62, which is before his FRA of 66, his monthly benefit is reduced to $1500. 75% of Tom's PIA of $2000 = $1500. In addition, since Tom collected his benefit early, he has permanently reduced Cindy's survivor benefit when Tom passes away to 82.5% of Tom's PIA of $2000 or $1650 per month. If Tom collects his benefit at FRA 66 he will receive his $2000 monthly benefit and Cindy's survivor benefit when Tom passes away will also be $2000. Finally, if Tom waits to collect his benefit at age 70, he will receive $2640 per month until he passes away and Cindy's survivor benefit will also be $2640. The Delayed Retirement Credits (DRCs) increase Tom's PIA of $2000 by 8% each year until he turns 70, a total increase of 32% ($2000 x 132% = $2640).

Cindy can collect her benefit early at age 62 and receive $1200 per month. Because Cindy collects at age 62 and not her Full Retirement Age (FRA) of 66, her Primary Insurance Amount (PIA) of $1600 is reduced. 75% of Cindy's PIA of $1600 = $1200. Also, Cindy is not able to collect a spousal benefit at age 62, even though Tom filed for his own earned benefit at 62. Why not? Because if she applies for spousal benefits before reaching FRA 66, the Social Security Administration requires her to apply for both her own earned benefit as well as the spousal benefit, and because her own earned benefit is greater than the spousal benefit, she will receive the greater of the two amounts, but not both. The spousal benefit is calculated by taking 50% of the higher earner's PIA and then subtracting the lower earner's PIA. 50% of Tom's PIA of $2000 = $1000. Cindy's own earned PIA is $1600 and is greater than 50% of Tom's PIA of $1000. Therefore, Cindy will not receive a spousal benefit. If Cindy waits to her FRA of 66 to collect her own benefit, she will receive her PIA of $1600. Again, Cindy will not receive a spousal benefit because her own earned benefit of $1600 is greater than the spousal benefit at FRA. Cindy's own earned PIA is $1600 and is greater than 50% of Tom's PIA (50% x $2000 = $1000). If Cindy waits to collect her earned benefit until age 70, her monthly benefit will increase by 32% because of Delayed Retirement Credits (DRCs) to $2112 per month ($1600 x 132% = $2112). Once again, there would be no spousal benefit because 50% of Tom's PIA is less than Cindy's PIA (50% of $2000 = $1000. $1000 is less than $1600).

Since Tom is the higher earning spouse, his earned benefits will continue not just until he passes away at age 72, but will also provide Cindy's survivor benefit until she passes away at age 92. This is an important point to remember because claiming Social Security benefits for a couple is not an individual decision, but a joint decision and should examine each spouse's life expectancy. **In general, the age at which the higher earning spouse should claim his/her Social Security benefit is based on the life expectancy of the lower earning spouse. And the age at which the lower earning spouse should claim his/her benefit is based on the life expectancy of the higher earning spouse.** The higher earning spouse Tom should claim his benefit based on his wife Cindy's life expectancy since his survivor benefit will continue after his death and provide Cindy with a higher income for her remainder years. For a married couple with a small difference in earned monthly Social Security benefits such as Tom and Cindy, Tom should claim his benefit based on Cindy's life expectancy of 92 and therefore take his Social Security benefit at age 70, even though he passes away at 72. In addition, Cindy should collect her benefit early based on Tom's shorter life expectancy since she will only collect reduced benefits for a relatively short amount of time until Tom passes away. She will then be eligible for Tom's survivor benefit. Now that we understand the relationship of life expectancy for a couple with a small difference in earned monthly Social Security benefits and the higher earning spouse's shorter than average life expectancy, we present the Collect Now Collect Later (CNCL) strategy.

Here's how it works: Cindy, the slightly lower earning spouse, collects her benefits at age 62 before her Full Retirement Age (FRA) and receives a reduced benefit of $1200 per month and Tom does nothing. Cindy's Primary Insurance Amount (PIA) is $1600, but she only receives 75% of this amount, or $1200, because she collects early at age 62. When Tom turns 66, his FRA, he files for spousal benefits only based on Cindy's record. The spousal benefit Tom collects is equal to 50% of Cindy's PIA or $800 (50% of Cindy's PIA of $1600 = $800). Tom's own earned benefit will receive Delayed Retirement Credits (DRCs) of 8% each year up to age 70 or a 32% total increase. At age 70, Tom collects his maximum benefit of $2640 (132% x $2000). When Tom passes away at age 72, Cindy will then receive a survivor benefit of $2640 for the rest of her life, which in this case is another 20 years! (Cindy's survivor benefit is the larger of her earned benefit or Tom's earned benefit based on his record.)

Let's look at the cumulative benefits for claiming at ages 62, 66 (FRA), 70 and then examine the strategy that maximizes the total cumulative Social Security benefits for a married couple with small difference in monthly earned Social Security benefits and shorter life expectancy:

	Collect at 62		Collect at 66		Collect at 70		Collect CNFAS			Collect CNCL		
Monthly Benefits													
Ages	**Tom**	**Cindy**	**Tom**	**Cindy**	**Tom**	**Cindy**	**Tom**	**Cindy**	**Spousal**	**Tom**	**Cindy**	**Spousal**
62/62	$1500	1200					$0	1200	0	$0	1200	
63/63	$1500	1200					$0	1200	0	$0	1200	
64/64	$1500	1200					$0	1200	0	$0	1200	
65/65	$1500	1200					$0	1200	0	$0	1200	
66/66	$1500	1200	$2000	1600			$0	1200	0	$0	1200	800
67/67	$1500	1200	$2000	1600			$0	1200	0	$0	1200	800
68/68	$1500	1200	$2000	1600			$0	1200	0	$0	1200	800
69/69	$1500	1200	$2000	1600			$0	1200	0	$0	1200	800
70/70	$1500	1200	$2000	1600	$2640	2112	$2640	1200	0	$2640	1200	0
71/71	$1500	1200	$2000	1600	$2640	2112	$2640	1200	0	$2640	1200	0
72/72	$0	1650	$0	2000	$0	2640	$0	2640	0	$0	2640	0
/73	$0	1650	$0	2000	$0	2640	$0	2640	0	$0	2640	0
/74	$0	1650	$0	2000	$0	2640	$0	2640	0	$0	2640	0
--	--	--	--	--	--	--	--	--	--	--	--	--
/91	$0	1650	$0	2000	$0	2640	$0	2640	0	$0	2640	0
/92	$0	0	$0	0	$0	0	$0	0	0	$0	0	0
Cumulative Combined Lifetime Benefits												
$720,000			$739,200		$747,648		$840,960			$879,360		

As you can see, the Collect Now Collect Later (CNCL) strategy generated the greatest amount of cumulative lifetime Social Security benefits for Tom and Cindy. **If Tom and Cindy simply took their benefits each at age 62 without thinking about or knowing how to maximize their benefits, they would have lost out on $159,360 in cumulative lifetime Social Security benefits that they worked hard for and earned!**

In our example, Tom and Cindy are both the same age. For a married couple with a relatively small difference in earned Social Security benefits, a shorter than average life expectancy for the higher earning spouse AND the spouses are different ages, the maximization strategies become more complicated. If the lower earning spouse Cindy was younger, it becomes even more important for Tom to delay his benefits past Full Retirement Age (FRA). However, the Collect Now Collect Later (CNCL) strategy may not generate the most cumulative lifetime income compared to other strategies. If Cindy is 5 years younger than Tom, she should collect her own earned benefit at age 62 which would allow Tom to collect a spousal benefit at age 67. Tom is 5 years older than Cindy and cannot receive a spousal benefit until Cindy collects her benefit. Since Tom is collecting a spousal only benefit, his own earned benefit will continue to receive Delayed Retirement Credits (DRCs) until he turns age 70. At age 70 he collects his earned benefit of $2640 until he passes away at age 72. Cindy would then receive Tom's survivor benefit of $2640 for 25 years! Even if Tom (the slightly higher earning spouse) was 5 years younger than Cindy (the slightly lower earning spouse), it still makes sense for Tom to delay collecting his Social Security benefits until age 70. Cindy could still collect her own individual benefits as early as age 62 and Tom could collect a spousal benefit only off of Cindy's earnings record when he turns 66. Tom would then switch and collect his own earned benefit at age 70 which received Delayed Retirement Credits. When Tom passes away at age 72, Cindy will then receive a survivor benefit of $2640 for the rest of her life, which in this case is another 15 years! (Cindy's survivor benefit is the larger of her earned benefit or Tom's earned benefit based on his record.)

These examples compare different ages at which you collect Social Security benefits and their cumulative totals. This is the easiest way to understand how to maximize your Social Security benefits. We call this the cumulative lifetime benefit approach. There are a few other factors that could change the decision when you decide to begin collecting your Social Security benefits. A present value calculation may be another method to calculate a claiming strategy. This is more complicated than the scope of Social Security Central

LLC's goal of keeping your Social Security maximization strategy simple. In a low interest rate environment (like that of 2012 when this book was written), the present value calculation approach won't change the outcome much, if any, from the cumulative lifetime benefit approach.

To get YOUR Social Security maximization strategy in just five minutes, visit www.socialsecuritycentral.com and use our proprietary Benefit Maximization Calculator. IT'S YOUR MONEY!

11 DEFINING YOU

STRATEGIES FOR DIVORCEES

If you are divorced, you can receive benefits from your ex-spouse's earnings record if: your marriage lasted for 10 years or more, you have been divorced for 2 or more years, you are currently unmarried, you are age 62 or older, your ex-spouse is 62 or older, your earned Social Security benefit is less than the benefits you would receive from your ex-spouse, and your ex-spouse is eligible for Social Security benefits. Your ex-spouse does not need to have applied for benefits for you to be eligible for spousal (ex-spousal) benefits. If you remarry, you may lose eligibility for ex-spousal benefits. If the new marriage ends in divorce, your previous ex-spousal benefits may start up again.

Your ex-spousal benefits will be calculated as 50% of your ex-spouse's Primary Insurance Amount (PIA). If you collect spousal benefits based on your ex-spouse's PIA prior to your Full Retirement Age (FRA), the spousal benefits will be reduced; you must also file for your own benefit at the same time reducing your benefit too. However, if you wait to collect your spousal benefit based on your ex-spouse's PIA at your FRA, you do not have to collect your own earned benefit. Your own earned benefit would receive Delayed Retirement Credits (DRCs) until you turn age 70. Spousal or ex-spousal benefits do not receive any DRCs, so there is no reason to delay their receipt beyond FRA.

If your ex-spouse is deceased, you may be eligible for survivor (ex-spouse) benefits. Your survivor benefits based on an ex-spouse are calculated the same as they would be for a current (married) spouse. However, the marriage must have lasted at least 10 years and you must be currently unmarried. If you are currently married, the marriage must have began after you reached age 60, and you must have been at least age 60 when your ex-spouse passed away. You can collect earlier than age 60 if disabled or caring for a child of the deceased ex-spouse under age 16. If you collect survivor (ex-spouse) benefits prior to your Full Retirement Age (FRA), they will be reduced.

DEFINING YOU: STRATEGIES FOR DIVORCEES   101

Many divorcees are unaware or forget that they may be able to collect a spousal benefit from their ex-spouse if the marriage lasted for at least 10 years, potentially leaving thousands of dollars on the table. If your own earned Primary Insurance Amount (PIA) is less than 50% of your ex-spouse's PIA, then you may be eligible to collect both your own earned benefit and a spousal (ex-spousal) benefit. Usually, you must provide the Social Security Administration with proof of your former marriage (e.g. marriage certificate, divorce decree) and your ex-spouse's Social Security number.

If you are divorced and single, the strategies to maximize cumulative benefits work similar to a married couple. The higher earning spouse should base his/her Social Security benefit collection age (age 62-70) on the greater of the two's life expectancies since the survivor benefit would continue to pay until the death of the surviving spouse. However, divorce complicates communication, cooperation, and therefore Social Security benefit claiming strategies to maximize cumulative lifetime benefits. Using the same strategies to maximize benefits as if the couple were still married will most likely not be possible, even though the strategies on paper would work the same. Therefore, the following strategies for divorced singles assume that communication between spouses does not exist.

That being the case, the most important factor to maximize your Social Security benefit is your own life expectancy. The ex-spousal benefit will simply add to your cumulative lifetime benefits, and the best way to maximize your benefits still depends on your life expectancy. In general, if you have a shorter than average life expectancy, you will maximize your cumulative lifetime benefits by taking both your own earned benefit as well as your ex-spousal benefit at age 62. It is important to note that the earnings test applies to your own earned benefits as well as spousal (ex-spousal) benefits if they are collected prior to Full Retirement Age (FRA). If your life expectancy is longer than average, then your cumulative lifetime benefits are maximized by delaying collection of your own earned benefit until age 70, but collecting a spousal (ex-spousal) benefit at your FRA. The logic behind this is spousal (ex-spousal) benefits do not receive Delayed Retirement Credits (DRCs) so there is no reason to delay collecting beyond your FRA.

> If you are divorced and single, the most important factor to maximize your Social Security benefit is your life expectancy. If your life expectancy is shorter than average, you are better off collecting benefits early at age 62. If your life expectancy is longer than average, you should delay collecting benefits until age 70.

We now go into a more in-depth view of maximizing benefits for a divorced-single individual. As we have stated before, your monthly Social Security benefit amount will depend on the age you decide to start collecting benefits. For example, let's assume your marriage of 25 years, ended 15 years ago. Your Primary Insurance Amount (PIA) at your Full Retirement Age (FRA) of 66 is $1000 per month and your ex-spouse (who is the same age as you) has a PIA at FRA of $2400. Since 50% of your ex-spouse's PIA is greater than your PIA, you will be eligible for a spousal (ex-spousal) benefit of $200 at your FRA. Here's how we calculated this: 50% of $2400 = $1200. $1200 – your PIA of $1000 = $200. $200 will be added to your own earned benefit of $1000 if you collect both benefits at FRA. Collecting the benefit early at age 62 would decrease your own earned benefit to $750 per month (you collect 75% of your PIA at age 62) and your spousal benefit would be reduced from $200 per month to $140. If your FRA is 66, you will receive only 70% of your spousal benefit if you collect at age 62. 70% of $200 = $140. Waiting to collect the benefit until age 70 would increase your own earned benefit to $1320 (you collect 132% of your PIA at age 70), but does not increase your spousal (ex-spousal) benefit of $200. Remember, spousal benefits do not receive Delayed Retirement Credits (DRCs). Therefore, in our examples below we will assume that spousal benefits are collected no later than FRA of 66.

As previously mentioned in Chapter 9, the Social Security Administration's actuaries calculate the factors that reduce or increase your own monthly benefits to be actuarially consistent. This means there will not be a significant difference in the cumulative benefits received if you pass away at age 80 regardless of when you begin collecting benefits. However, if you are divorced and unmarried, eligibility and collection of an ex-spousal benefit in addition to your own individual benefit may have the affect of lowering the actuarially consistent age to 76. For example, using the numbers in the example above ($750 per month at age 62, $1000 at age 66 and $1320 at age 70) your cumulative benefits collected up to age 76 are as follows:

Cumulative Lifetime Benefits Through Age 76					
Collect at age 62		Collect at age 66 (FRA)		Collect at age 70	
Your Benefit	Ex-spousal	Your Benefit	Ex-spousal	Your Benefit	Ex-spousal
$126,000	$23,520	$120,000	$24,000	$95,040	$57,600
Total: $149,520		Total: $144,000		Total: $152,640	

As you can see, these options are all approximately the same cumulative dollar amount, with collection at age 70 providing you slightly more. However, both your own earned benefits and spousal (ex-spousal) benefit cumulative amounts will change considerably based on your individual life expectancy. Let's assume, that you are not in good health and your life expectancy is only 72. Based on this lower life expectancy, collecting your Social Security benefits at age 62 would maximize your cumulative benefits:

Cumulative Lifetime Benefits Through Age 72					
Collect at age 62		Collect at age 66 (FRA)		Collect at age 70	
Your Benefit	Ex-spousal	Your Benefit	Ex-spousal	Your Benefit	Ex-spousal
$90,000	$16,800	$72,000	$14,400	$31,680	$57,600
Total: $106,800		Total: $86,400		Total: $89,280	

Let's assume, that you are in good health and have longevity in your family history. Perhaps one of your parents is still alive at age 95. Let's assume that you expect to live a long life as well, and we change your life expectancy to age 95. Based on this longer life expectancy, collecting your Social Security benefits at age 70 would maximize your cumulative benefits:

Cumulative Lifetime Benefits Through Age 95					
Collect at age 62		Collect at age 66 (FRA)		Collect at age 70	
Your Benefit	Ex-spousal	Your Benefit	Ex-spousal	Your Benefit	Ex-spousal
$297,000	$55,440	$348,000	$69,600	$396,000	$57,600
Total: $352,440		Total: $417,600		Total: $453,600	

As you can see, collecting your benefits and spousal (ex-spousal) benefits early at age 62, but having a longer than average life expectancy can cost you thousands of dollars. In this example, it would have cost you $101,160!

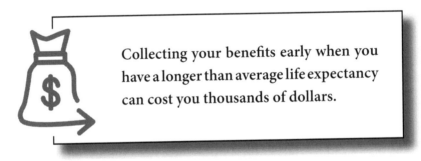

Collecting your benefits early when you have a longer than average life expectancy can cost you thousands of dollars.

Finally, let's look at what the RP-2000 Mortality Table calculates our average life expectancy based on current age and gender:

Single Male		Single Female	
Age	Lives to	Age	Lives to
62	85	62	88

Cumulative Lifetime Benefits Through Age 85 (Male)					
Collect at age 62		Collect at age 66 (FRA)		Collect at age 70	
Your Benefit	Ex-spousal	Your Benefit	Ex-spousal	Your Benefit	Ex-spousal
$207,000	$38,640	$228,000	$45,600	$237,600	$57,600
Total: $245,640		Total: $273,600		Total: $295,200	

Cumulative Lifetime Benefits Through Age 88 (Female)					
Collect at age 62		Collect at age 66 (FRA)		Collect at age 70	
Your Benefit	Ex-spousal	Your Benefit	Ex-spousal	Your Benefit	Ex-spousal
$234,000	$43,680	$264,000	$52,800	$285,120	$57,600
Total: $277,680		Total: $316,800		Total: $342,720	

Keep in mind that a survivor (ex-spouse) benefit could add to the cumulative lifetime Social Security benefit totals and perhaps change some of the strategies on how to claim benefits. However, we are assuming that your death occurs prior to the death of your ex-spouse.

So let's summarize the best strategy to maximize your total cumulative benefits for a divorced-single individual that does not have any communication or cooperation from an ex-spouse. If your life expectancy is shorter than average, you are better off collecting benefits early at age 62. If your life expectancy is longer than average you should delay collecting benefits until age 70. Keep in mind that these are general strategies. The size of your individual benefit relative to your ex-spouse's benefit may also factor into your claiming strategy. In some cases, collecting your individual benefit and ex-spousal benefit at your Full Retirement Age (FRA) of 66 will yield the same cumulative amount as collecting your ex-spousal benefit only at FRA 66, and then collecting your own individual benefit at age 70. For example, let's assume that your Primary Insurance Amount (PIA) at your Full Retirement Age (FRA) of 66 is $700 per month and your ex-spouse (who is the same age as you) has a PIA at FRA of $2400. Since 50% of your ex-spouse's PIA is greater than your PIA, you will be eligible for a spousal (ex-spousal) benefit of $500 at your FRA. Here's how we calculated this: 50% of $2400 = $1200. $1200 – your PIA of $700 = $500. $500 will be added to your own earned benefit of $700 if you collect both benefits at FRA for a total of $1200 per month. If you collect your ex-spousal benefit only at age 66, you will receive the same $1200 (50% of $2400 = $1200). Switching to collect your individual benefit at age 70 will increase your own earned benefit to $924 (you collect 132% of your PIA at age 70), but this amount is still less than the ex-spousal benefit you were receiving in the amount of $1200. Therefore, a $276 ex-spousal benefit will be added to your own benefit of $924 for a total amount of $1200 per month.

Finally, the survivor (ex-spouse) benefit can be used to help maximize your individual divorced-single cumulative Social Security benefits once your ex-spouse has passed away. As we stated earlier, divorce complicates communication, cooperation, and therefore complicates strategies to maximize cumulative lifetime benefits. Using the same maximization strategies as if the couple were still married will most likely not be possible, even though on paper the strategies would work the same. We can't assume that a higher earning ex-spouse will defer his/her own earned Social Security benefit to age 70 to maximize the survivor benefit for his/her ex-spouse. However, if the death of an ex-spouse occurs prior to your turning age 60 or prior to claiming your own earned benefit, we can use the survivor (ex-spouse) benefit to help maximize your cumulative lifetime Social Security benefits. You will receive the larger of either your own earned benefit or the survivor (ex-spouse) benefit. Also important to note: a widow/er survivor's Full Retirement Age (FRA) is different than an individual worker's FRA (see Survivor Full Retirement Age Table in Chapter 3).

OPTION A—
DIVORCED & WIDOWED (UNMARRIED) W/BIG DIFFERENCE IN EARNED BENEFIT & SURVIVOR BENEFIT

PROPOSED SSC STRATEGY =
Collect Now Survivor Later (CNSL)

Tom and Cindy, both the same age, divorced after 25 years of marriage and have been divorced for the last 15 years. Tom had been the primary income earner while they were married and Cindy had stayed home to raise their children. After their divorce, Cindy went back into the work force. Recently, Tom passed away at age 60. Cindy is single throughout retirement and passes away at age 88 (passes away the month she turns 88). Cindy's Primary Insurance Amount (PIA) is expected to be $900 per month and her survivor (ex-spouse) benefit based on Tom's (ex-spouse) earnings record at her Full Retirement Age (FRA) is expected to be $2000. Cindy can collect a survivor's (ex-spouse) benefit as early as age 60, but it will be reduced for every month taken prior to Cindy's survivor FRA. Cindy's own earned monthly benefit will never grow to more than $1188. Cindy's PIA of $900 will receive 8% each year in Delayed Retirement Credits (DRCs) until age 70 or a 32% total increase if she doesn't collect until then. $900 x 132% = $1188. In addition, since Tom passed away before earning any DRCs on his own earned benefit, the survivor (ex-spouse) benefit will never exceed his PIA of $2000. Finally, it is important to remember that you can collect the greater of your own earned benefit or a survivor benefit, but you cannot collect them at the same time. Therefore, the strategy that maximizes Cindy's cumulative lifetime Social Security benefits is to collect her own earned benefit early at age 62 (Cindy will receive 75% of her PIA of $900 because she is collecting early, 75% x $900 = $675) and switch to her survivor (ex-spouse) benefit at her FRA of 66. This is referred to as the Collect Now Survivor Later (CNSL) strategy. Below are Cindy's options based on age, assuming that her own earned benefit is quite a bit smaller than her survivor (ex-spouse) benefit, highlighting the strategy that maximizes her cumulative lifetime Social Security benefits:

	Collect Survivor at 60		Collect at 62		Collect at 66 (FRA)		Collect at 70		Collect CNSL	
Ages	**Cindy**	**Survivor**	**Cindy**	**Survivor**	**Cindy**	**Survivor**	**Cindy**	**Survivor**	**Cindy**	**Survivor**
60	$0	1430	$0	0	$0	0	$0	0	$0	0
61	$0	1430	$0	0	$0	0	$0	0	$0	0
62	$0	1430	$0	1620	$0	0	$0	0	$675	0
63	$0	1430	$0	1620	$0	0	$0	0	$675	0
64	$0	1430	$0	1620	$0	0	$0	0	$675	0
65	$0	1430	$0	1620	$0	0	$0	0	$675	0
66	$0	1430	$0	1620	$0	2000	$0	0	$0	2000
67	$0	1430	$0	1620	$0	2000	$0	0	$0	2000
68	$0	1430	$0	1620	$0	2000	$0	0	$0	2000
69	$0	1430	$0	1620	$0	2000	$0	0	$0	2000
70	$0	1430	$0	1620	$0	2000	$0	$2000	$0	2000
77	$0	1430	$0	1620	$0	2000	$0	$2000	$0	2000
--	--	--	--	--	--	--	--	--	--	--
88	$0	1430	$0	1620	$0	2000	$0	$2000	$0	2000
89	$0	0	$0	0	$0	0	$0	0	$0	0
Cumulative Combined Lifetime Benefits										
$480,480			$505,440		$528,000		$432,000		**$560,400**	

As you can see, the Collect Now Survivor Later (CNSL) strategy generated the greatest amount of cumulative lifetime Social Security benefits for Cindy. This is based on her own earned benefit amount and survivor (ex-spouse) benefit earned off her ex-spouse Tom's record. **If Cindy simply took her survivor (ex-spouse) benefit at age 60 without thinking about or knowing how to maximize her benefits, she would have lost out on $79,920 in cumulative lifetime Social Security benefits that she worked hard for and earned!**

OPTION B—
DIVORCED & WIDOWED (UNMARRIED) W/SMALL DIFFERENCE IN EARNED BENEFIT & SURVIVOR BENEFIT

PROPOSED SSC STRATEGY =
Survivor Now Collect Later (SNCL)

Tom and Cindy, both the same age, divorced after 25 years of marriage and have been divorced for the last 15 years. Tom and Cindy both had successful careers. Recently, Tom passed away at age 60. Cindy lives a single retirement and passes away at age 88 (passed away the month she turns 88). Cindy's Primary Insurance Amount (PIA) is expected to be $1800 per month and her survivor (ex-spouse) benefit based off Tom's (ex-spouse) earnings record at her Full Retirement Age (FRA) is expected to be $2000. Cindy can collect a survivor's (ex-spousal) benefit as early as age 60, but it will be reduced for every month taken prior to Cindy's survivor FRA. Cindy can delay her own earned monthly benefit, which will grow to $2376 by age 70. Her PIA of $1800 will receive 8% Delayed Retirement Credits (DRCs) each year until age 70 or a 32% increase if she doesn't collect it until then. $1800 x 132% = $2376. In addition, since Tom passed away before earning any DRCs on his own earned benefit, the survivor (ex-spouse) benefit will never exceed his PIA of $2000. Delaying Cindy's own earned benefit to age 70 ($2376) would produce a larger monthly amount at that age than the survivor (ex-spouse) benefit of $2000. Finally, it is important to remember that you can collect the greater of your own earned benefit or a survivor benefit, but you cannot collect them at the same time. Therefore, the strategy that maximizes Cindy's cumulative lifetime Social Security benefits is to collect her survivor (ex-spouse) benefit at age 60 (Cindy will receive 71.5% of her survivor (ex-spouse) benefit of $2000 because she is collecting it at age 60. 71.5% x $2000 = $1430) and switch to her own earned benefit at age 70. This is referred to as the Survivor Now Collect Later (SNCL) strategy. Below are Cindy's options based on age assuming that her earned benefit is similar to her survivor (ex-spouse) benefit, highlighting the strategy that maximizes her cumulative lifetime Social Security benefits:

Monthly Benefits									
Collect Survivor at 60		Collect at 62		Collect at 66 (FRA)		Collect at 70		Collect SNCL	
Ages	Cindy	Survivor	Cindy	Survivor	Cindy	Survivor	Cindy	Survivor	Cindy	Survivor
60	$0	1430	$0	0	$0	0	$0	0	$0	1430
61	$0	1430	$0	0	$0	0	$0	0	$0	1430
62	$0	1430	$0	1620	$0	0	$0	0	$0	1430
63	$0	1430	$0	1620	$0	0	$0	0	$0	1430
64	$0	1430	$0	1620	$0	0	$0	0	$0	1430
65	$0	1430	$0	1620	$0	0	$0	0	$0	1430
66	$0	1430	$0	1620	$0	2000	$0	0	$0	1430
67	$0	1430	$0	1620	$0	2000	$0	0	$0	1430
68	$0	1430	$0	1620	$0	2000	$0	0	$0	1430
69	$0	1430	$0	1620	$0	2000	$0	0	$0	1430
70	$0	1430	$0	1620	$0	2000	$2376	0	$2376	0
77	$0	1430	$0	1620	$0	2000	$2376	0	$2376	0
--	--	--	--	--	--	--	--	--	--	--
88	$0	1430	$0	1620	$0	2000	$2376	0	$2376	0
89	$0	0	$0	0	$0	0	$0	0	$0	0
Cumulative Combined Lifetime Benefits									
$480,480		$505,440		$528,000		$513,216		$684,816	

As you can see, the Survivor Now Collect Later (SNCL) strategy generated the greatest amount of cumulative lifetime Social Security benefits for Cindy, based on her own earned benefit amount and survivor (ex-spouse) benefit earned off her ex-spouse Tom's record. **If Cindy simply took her survivor (ex-spouse) benefit at age 60 without thinking about or knowing how to maximize her benefits, she would have lost out on $204,336 in cumulative lifetime Social Security benefits that she worked hard for and earned!**

These examples compare different ages at which you collect Social Security benefits and their cumulative totals. This is the easiest way to understand how to maximize your Social Security benefits. We call this the cumulative lifetime benefit approach. There are a few other factors that could change the decision when you decide to begin collecting your Social Security benefits. A present value calculation may be another method to calculate a claiming strategy. This is more complicated than the scope of Social Security Central LLC's goal of keeping your Social Security maximization strategy simple. In a low interest rate environment (like that of 2012 when this book was written), the present value calculation approach won't change the outcome much, if any, from the cumulative lifetime benefit approach.

To get YOUR Social Security maximization strategy in just five minutes, visit www.socialsecuritycentral.com and use our proprietary Benefit Maximization Calculator. IT'S YOUR MONEY!

12 DEFINING YOU

STRATEGIES FOR WIDOWS/WIDOWERS

If you are a widow or widower, you may be eligible to receive benefits from your deceased spouse. To be eligible, your marriage must have lasted for 9 months or longer, you must be unmarried or remarried after turning age 60, you must be age 60 or older, your earned Social Security benefit must be less than the survivor benefit you would receive from your deceased spouse's earnings record, and your deceased spouse must be eligible for Social Security benefits. Your deceased spouse does not need to have applied for benefits for you to be eligible for survivor benefits. If you remarry prior to age 60, you may lose eligibility for survivor benefits. If the new marriage ends in divorce, your survivor benefits from your previous deceased spouse may start up again. You may collect survivor benefits as early as age 60, but because you collected them prior to your survivor Full Retirement Age (FRA) (which is different than your individual FRA—see Survivor Full Retirement Age Table in Chapter 3), they will be prorated monthly between age 60 and your survivor FRA. You can collect earlier than age 60 if disabled or caring for a child of the deceased spouse under age 16. Also, survivor benefits collected prior to FRA may be subject to the earnings test and withheld. The Social Security Administration pays all widows/ers a one-time lump-sum death benefit payment of $255.

The amount of monthly survivor benefits to which a widow/er is eligible depends on when the deceased spouse collected his/her own earned individual benefits. If the deceased spouse never collected monthly Social Security benefits, then the widow/er may be eligible to receive 100% of the deceased spouse's Primary Insurance Amount (PIA). However, if the widow/er collects the survivor benefit prior to his/her own survivor Full Retirement Age (FRA), then the survivor benefit will be reduced for every month it was collected early.

If the deceased spouse passed away prior to collecting monthly Social Security benefits and had earned Delayed Retirement Credits (DRCs), then the widow/er may be eligible to receive those DRCs on the survivor benefit. For example, if a deceased spouse had not yet collected monthly Social Security benefits, but passed away at the age of 68, the survivor benefit may include the two years of DRCs at 8% per year for a total of 16% more than the deceased spouse's Primary Insurance Amount (PIA). However, the survivor benefit will still be reduced, including any DRCs the deceased spouse earned, if the surviving spouse collects survivor benefits prior to his/her survivor Full Retirement Age (FRA).

If the deceased spouse had collected his/her own earned benefit early before passing away, the widow/er's survivor benefit will be permanently reduced. This is why it is important to remember that for couples, the decision to collect an earned monthly Social Security benefit should be a joint decision, not an individual one because it can have a lasting impact on the surviving spouse and cost thousands of dollars in lost benefits.

Remember, for couples, the decision of when to collect Social Security should be a joint decision, not an individual one, because it can have a lasting impact on the surviving spouse and cost thousands of dollars in lost benefits.

Finally, as a widow/er if you haven't yet started collecting your own earned monthly Social Security benefit, you may choose to collect a survivor's benefit while allowing your own earned benefit to increase in value with Delayed Retirement Credits (DRCs) of 8% per year until age 70. You are then allowed to switch from collecting your survivor benefit to your own earned benefit if it produces a higher monthly benefit.

If you're already collecting your own earned monthly Social Security benefit and you lose your spouse, you may collect the monthly survivor benefit right away or delay collecting it. If your own earned benefit is less than your survivor benefit, the Social Security Administration will simply add the difference to your own earned benefit, bringing the total value up to the survivor benefit. For example, if your own earned benefit at your Full Retirement Age (FRA) is $1600 per month and you decide to collect your survivor benefit of $2000 at your survivor FRA (which is different than your individual FRA), then the Social Security Administration will add $400 to your own earned benefit of $1600 to equal $2000. 100% of $2000 survivor benefit – $1600 your own earned monthly benefit = $400. $400 is added to your own earned $1600 benefit. If your own earned benefit is greater than your survivor benefit, there will not be an adjustment made to your monthly benefits, but you will still receive a one-time lump-sum death benefit payment of $255.

Maximizing your cumulative monthly Social Security benefits as a widow/er ideally follows the same maximization strategies as a married couple, which we've previously discussed. Again, it is important to remember that for couples, the decision to collect an earned monthly Social Security benefit should be a joint decision, not an individual one, because it can have a lasting impact on the surviving spouse and cost thousands of dollars in lost benefits. Ideally, couples will have planned their Social Security maximization strategy before the loss of either spouse. However, this may not always be the case as the loss of a spouse can occur unexpectedly. We will examine various strategies on how to maximize your cumulative monthly combined (your own earned benefit plus survivor benefit) Social Security benefits as a widow/er assuming the death of a spouse has already occurred. We will also make the assumption that you will live to your average life expectancy once you attain age 62. That means for men that reach age 62, the average life expectancy is 85 and for women the reach age 62, their average life expectancy is 88. Once the death of a spouse occurs, the single greatest factor to maximize your benefits is your individual life expectancy. Strategies will also depend on whether the deceased spouse was collecting individual benefits prior to the death occurring. In general, if your life expectancy is less than age 80 after the loss of a spouse, you will maximize your cumulative lifetime benefits by collecting the greater of either your own earned benefit or your survivor benefit as early as possible. The Social Security Administration does not allow you to collect both your own earned benefit and your survivor benefit at the same time. If you were already collecting your own earned benefit, check to see if the survivor benefit will increase your monthly Social Security benefit. If that's the case, the Social Security Administration will combine the benefits to equal the greater survivor benefit. It is important to note that the earnings test applies to your own earned benefits as well as your survivor benefits if they are collected prior to Full Retirement Age (FRA).

In general, if your life expectancy is less than age 80 after the loss of a spouse, you will maximize your cumulative lifetime benefits by collecting the greater of either your own earned benefit or your survivor benefit as early as possible.

Option A—
Widow/er (Unmarried) w/Big Difference In Earned Benefit & Survivor Benefit

PROPOSED SSC STRATEGY =
Collect Now Survivor Later (CNSL)

Tom and Cindy, both the same age, were married for 35 years. Tom was the primary income earner while they were married and Cindy stayed home to raise their children. After their kids were grown, Cindy went back into the work force. Recently, Tom passed away at age 60. Cindy lives a single retirement and passes away at age 88 (passes away the month she turns 88). Cindy's Primary Insurance Amount (PIA) is expected to be $900 per month and her survivor benefit based off Tom's own earnings record at her survivor FRA is expected to be $2000. Cindy can collect a survivor benefit as early as age 60, but it will be reduced for every month taken prior to Cindy's survivor FRA. Cindy's own earned monthly benefit will never grow to more than $1188. Her PIA of $900 will receive 8% Delayed Retirement Credits (DRCs) each year until age 70 or a 32% increase if she doesn't collect it until then. $900 x 132% = $1188. In addition, since Tom passed away before earning any Delayed Retirement Credits (DRCs) on his own earned benefit, the survivor benefit will never exceed his PIA of $2000. Finally, it is important to remember that you can collect the greater of your own earned benefit or a survivor benefit, but you cannot collect them at the same time. Therefore, the strategy that maximizes Cindy's cumulative lifetime Social Security benefits is to collect her own earned benefit at age 62 (Cindy will receive 75% of her PIA of $900 because she is collecting it at age 62. 75% of $900 = $675.) and switch to her survivor benefit at her FRA of 66. This is referred to as the Collect Now Survivor Later (CNSL) strategy. Below are Cindy's options assuming that her own earned benefit is quite a bit smaller than her survivor benefit, highlighting the strategy that maximizes her cumulative lifetime Social Security benefits:

Monthly Benefits									
Collect Survivor at 60		Collect at 62		Collect at 66 (FRA)		Collect at 70		Collect CNSL	
Ages	Cindy	Survivor	Cindy	Survivor	Cindy	Survivor	Cindy	Survivor	Cindy	Survivor
60	$0	1430	$0	0	$0	0	$0	0	$0	0
61	$0	1430	$0	0	$0	0	$0	0	$0	0
62	$0	1430	$0	1620	$0	0	$0	0	$675	0
63	$0	1430	$0	1620	$0	0	$0	0	$675	0
64	$0	1430	$0	1620	$0	0	$0	0	$675	0
65	$0	1430	$0	1620	$0	0	$0	0	$675	0
66	$0	1430	$0	1620	$0	2000	$0	0	$0	2000
67	$0	1430	$0	1620	$0	2000	$0	0	$0	2000
68	$0	1430	$0	1620	$0	2000	$0	0	$0	2000
69	$0	1430	$0	1620	$0	2000	$0	0	$0	2000
70	$0	1430	$0	1620	$0	2000	$0	$2000	$0	2000
77	$0	1430	$0	1620	$0	2000	$0	$2000	$0	2000
--	--	--	--	--	--	--	--	--	--	--
88	$0	1430	$0	1620	$0	2000	$0	$2000	$0	2000
89	$0	0	$0	0	$0	0	$0	0	$0	0
Cumulative Combined Lifetime Benefits									
$480,480		$505,440		$528,000		$432,000		$560,400	

As you can see, the Collect Now Survivor Later (CNSL) strategy generated the greatest amount of cumulative lifetime Social Security benefits for Cindy, based off her own earned benefit amount and survivor benefit earned off her deceased spouse Tom's record. **If Cindy simply took her survivor benefit at age 60 without thinking about or knowing how to maximize her benefits, she would have lost out on $79,920 in cumulative lifetime Social Security benefits that she worked hard for and earned!**

OPTION B—
WIDOW/ER (UNMARRIED) W/SMALL DIFFERENCE IN EARNED
BENEFIT & SURVIVOR BENEFIT

PROPOSED SSC STRATEGY =
Survivor Now Collect Later (SNCL)

Tom and Cindy, both the same age were married for 35 years. Tom and Cindy both had successful careers. Recently, Tom passed away at age 60. Cindy lives a single retirement and passes away at age 88 (passing away the month she turns 88). Cindy's Primary Insurance Amount (PIA) is expected to be $1800 per month and her survivor benefit based off Tom's earnings record at her Full Retirement Age (FRA) is expected to be $2000. Cindy can collect a survivor benefit as early as age 60, but it will be reduced for every month taken prior to Cindy's survivor FRA. Cindy can delay her own earned monthly benefit, which will grow to $2376 by age 70. Her PIA of $1800 will receive 8% Delayed Retirement Credits (DRCs) each year until age 70 or a 32% increase if she doesn't collect it until then. $1800 x 132% = $2376. In addition, since Tom passed away before earning any DRCs on his own earned benefit, the survivor benefit will never exceed his PIA of $2000. Delaying Cindy's own earned benefit to age 70 ($2376) will produce a larger monthly amount at age 70 than the survivor benefit of $2000. Finally, it is important to remember that you can collect the greater of your own earned benefit or a survivor benefit, but you cannot collect them at the same time. Therefore, the strategy that maximizes Cindy's cumulative lifetime Social Security benefits is to collect her survivor benefit at age 60 (Cindy's will receive 71.5% of her survivor benefit of $2000 because she is collecting it at age 60. 71.5% x $2000 = $1430.) and switch to her own earned benefit at age 70. This is referred to as the Survivor Now Collect Later (SNCL) strategy. Below are Cindy's options assuming that her own earned benefit is similar in monthly value to her survivor benefit, highlighting the strategy that maximizes her cumulative lifetime Social Security benefits:

	Monthly Benefits									
	Collect Survivor at 60		Collect at 62		Collect at 66 (FRA)		Collect at 70		Collect SNCL	
Ages	Cindy	Survivor	Cindy	Survivor	Cindy	Survivor	Cindy	Survivor	Cindy	Survivor
60	$0	1430	$0	0	$0	0	$0	0	$0	1430
61	$0	1430	$0	0	$0	0	$0	0	$0	1430
62	$0	1430	$0	1620	$0	0	$0	0	$0	1430
63	$0	1430	$0	1620	$0	0	$0	0	$0	1430
64	$0	1430	$0	1620	$0	0	$0	0	$0	1430
65	$0	1430	$0	1620	$0	0	$0	0	$0	1430
66	$0	1430	$0	1620	$0	2000	$0	0	$0	1430
67	$0	1430	$0	1620	$0	2000	$0	0	$0	1430
68	$0	1430	$0	1620	$0	2000	$0	0	$0	1430
69	$0	1430	$0	1620	$0	2000	$0	0	$0	1430
70	$0	1430	$0	1620	$0	2000	$2376	0	$2376	0
77	$0	1430	$0	1620	$0	2000	$2376	0	$2376	0
--	--	--	--	--	--	--	--	--	--	--
88	$0	1430	$0	1620	$0	2000	$2376	0	$2376	0
89	$0	0	$0	0	$0	0	$0	0	$0	0
Cumulative Combined Lifetime Benefits										
$480,480		$505,440		$528,000		$513,216		$684,816		

As you can see, the Survivor Now Collect Later (SNCL) strategy generated the greatest amount of cumulative lifetime Social Security benefits for Cindy, based off her own earned benefit amount and survivor benefit earned off her deceased spouse Tom's record. **If Cindy simply took her survivor benefit at age 60 without thinking about or knowing how to maximize her benefits, she would have lost out on $204,336 in cumulative lifetime Social Security benefits that she worked hard for and earned!**

To maximize cumulative monthly Social Security benefits as a widow/er, assuming average life expectancy and assuming that the surviving spouse has not yet collected his/her own earned benefit, consider the following:

Follow these rules of thumb to maximize widow/er cumulative Social Security benefits:

Compare the worth of your own earned benefit at age 70, including Delayed Retirement Credits (DRCs), to the worth of your survivor benefit from your deceased spouse's earnings at age 70. Remember, unless your deceased spouse had earned DRCs on his/her own benefit prior to death, a survivor benefit will not receive DRCs.

1. If your own earned benefit is expected to be greater than your survivor benefit earned off your deceased spouse's earnings at age 70, then you should collect the survivor benefit now and collect your own earned benefit at age 70. This is our Survivor Now Collect Later (SNCL) strategy.

2. If your own earned benefit is expected to be less than your survivor benefit earned off your deceased spouse's earnings at age 70, then you should collect your own earned benefit now and switch to collect your survivor benefit at your Full Retirement Age (FRA) of 66. This is our Collect Now Survivor Later (CNSL) strategy.

Finally, if the loss of a spouse occurs after the widow/er has collected his/her own earned benefit, then the surviving spouse should collect the survivor benefit right away.

These examples compare different ages at which you collect Social Security benefits and their cumulative totals. This is the easiest way to understand how to maximize your Social Security benefits. We call this the cumulative lifetime benefit approach. There are a few other factors that could change the decision when you decide to begin collecting your Social Security benefits. A present value calculation may be another method to calculate a claiming strategy. This is more complicated than the scope of Social Security Central LLC's goal of keeping your Social Security maximization strategy simple. In a low interest rate environment (like that of 2012 when this book was written), the present value calculation approach won't change the outcome much, if any, from the cumulative lifetime benefit approach.

To get YOUR Social Security maximization strategy in just five minutes, visit www.socialsecuritycentral.com and use our proprietary Benefit Maximization Calculator. IT'S YOUR MONEY!

13 THE CULMINIATION

RECAPPING YOUR CUSTOMIZED MAXIMIZATION STRATEGY

Hopefully, you now have a better understanding of the various Social Security maximization strategies for singles, married couples, divorcees, and widows/widowers. We covered the most common scenarios and demonstrated how different collection strategies can add thousands of dollars to your cumulative lifetime benefits. You've paid into Social Security for years. Don't you owe it to yourself to maximize your benefits when the time comes? IT'S YOUR MONEY!

Maximizing your income in retirement will better help you maintain your ideal retirement lifestyle and help you keep your financial independance. However, everyone's situation is unique, and it's important to keep in mind that the strategies outlined are clues to help you find the answer that is right for you. The strategies outlined were created under the guidelines and rules for Social Security at the time of publishing. Congress has made changes in the past to these rules and can do so going forward.

To help you figure out which Social Security maximization strategy is best for you and your family, we have created a proprietary Benefit Maximization Calculator. Visit www.socialsecuritycentral.com and use this must-have tool to calculate your maximum cumulative lifetime Social Security benefit.

PART THREE

SOCIAL SECURITY CENTRAL LLC HELPS YOU FILE WITH THE SSA

If you understand the process and do some planning to maximize your benefits, applying for Social Security is not difficult. It will be a much smoother process now that you understand the strategies to collect and are confident in your education when asking questions of the Social Security Administration (SSA). Social Security benefits can be applied for in three different ways: in person at your local SSA office, over the phone with a SSA claims representative, or online at the SSA website (www.ssa.gov). It is up to the SSA to approve your application, and they may even provide any owed back payments when your application is complete and approved.

14 How to File

No matter what type of Social Security benefit you are applying for (your own earned monthly benefit, spousal/ex-spousal benefit, survivor benefit, disability, etc.), the Social Security Administration (SSA) will want certain documentation to prove your eligibility. These documents are used to prove your age, recent earnings and, if need be, proof of citizenship. You will want to gather and provide the following documents:

- Your Social Security card or a record with your Social Security number on it

- Your original or certified birth certificate

- Your most recent tax return and/or earnings statement / W-2

- Proof of U.S. Citizenship (if you were not born in the United States)

- Military discharge papers (if applicable)

These documents must be originals or certified copies from the issuing agency. If you don't have all of your documentation, you should still apply for your benefits when the time is right for your individual situation. You can provide the documentation you have and go back and provide any missing documents to the SSA at a later date. In some cases, the Social Security Administration can help you locate some of the needed documentation by contacting your state Bureau of Vital Statistics.

If you are applying for a spousal benefit, ex-spousal benefit or survivor benefit, you may need additional documentation, which may include:

- Marriage certificate

- Death certificate

- Divorce decree

- Spouse's, ex-spouse's or deceased spouse's Social Security number

If you choose to have your benefits paid through direct deposit, you will also need your bank's name, your account number and your bank's routing number (located at the bottom of your checks). This is important to remember because new Social Security applicants must receive their monthly payments either electronically via direct deposit into a bank account or onto a Direct Express prepaid debit card, which is set up for individuals without a bank account. Those already receiving monthly Social Security benefits will have to shift to one of these two options in the near future. Bottom line, the check is no longer going to be in the mail.

> The check is no longer in the mail. Social Security benefits are now delivered via direct deposit or onto a prepaid debit card.

15 When to File

When Should You Apply?

You may file for your individual benefits up to three months before you want your monthly benefits to start. If you are applying before your Full Retirement Age (FRA), you can apply more than three months before the month you turn age 62. Because the process for applying for benefits and determining your eligibility may take some time, it is recommend that you do not procrastinate and use this three month period once you determine the right strategy and age that maximizes your cumulative benefits. Don't worry if can't find all of your necessary documentation. You should still apply knowing that the Social Security Administration (SSA) may help you locate some of the information required. In some cases, you may receive back payments owed to you when your application is approved. However, you usually are not compensated for monthly benefits owed to you just because you forgot to apply. If you are applying for survivor benefits, you may apply as early as the same month the deceased spouse passes away. That being said, you should apply for survivor benefits based on your age and your strategy to maximize your cumulative benefits, which may not be in the same month your spouse passes away.

When Do You Receive Your First Monthly Social Security Payment?

Generally speaking, your payment is due in the month following your birthday, unless your birthday is on the 1st or 2nd of the month. If that is the case, your payment is due in the same month. The actual payment is made to you the month after it is due. Finally, for birthdays that fall on the 1st through the 10th of the month, your payment is made the 2nd Wednesday of every month. If your birthday falls on the 11th through the 20th, your payment is made the 3rd Wednesday of the month. And if your birthday falls on the 21st through the 31st, your payment is made on the 4th Wednesday of the month. For example, if your birthday is March 18, then it is due in April and paid in May. Specifically, it will begin to be paid the 3rd Wednesday of May and will be paid the 3rd Wednesday of every month going forward.

16 Where to File

Where Should I Apply For My Social Security Benefits?

You are able to apply for your monthly Social Security benefits with a Social Security Administration (SSA) claims representative in person at your local SSA office, over the phone, or online at the SSA website (www.ssa.gov). It is recommended that you apply in person at the local SSA office to conduct your claims interview. When you are ready to apply for your benefits, you may walk in to your local SSA office or you may schedule an appointment in advance over the phone by calling the SSA's toll free number 800-722-1213, Monday through Friday from 7am to 7pm. When you call, ask the service representative any questions you have about your Social Security benefits and confirm with them the documentation that you will need. Then have them schedule an appointment for you to apply for benefits with a claims representative. We recommend you apply in person, but you can also schedule a phone appointment with a claims representative to apply if this is more feasible for your personal situation. Mondays and Fridays tend to be busiest for the SSA and could cause excessive wait times in person or over the phone. To locate your nearest SSA office, call their toll free number 800-722-1213 or go to the Social Security Administration website (www.ssa.gov) and click on the link *"Locate a Social Security Office"*. The direct URL to the SSA office locator is: https://secure.ssa.gov/apps6z/FOLO/fo001.jsp.

You may also apply for certain Social Security benefits online at the Social Security Administration (SSA) website, www.ssa.gov. On the top left corner of the webpage, click on the link *"Apply Online For Retirement Benefits"*. If you do not complete your Social Security application in one sitting, you may save your work and come back to it at a later time. You may also have to provide additional documentations to the SSA. If you make a mistake on your application or you change your mind about the application you filed online for your benefits, you need to contact the SSA right away. Please note that filling out an application online without understanding the process or having the guidance of a Social Security Administration claims representative may lead to errors.

So now that you understand how, when and where to apply for your benefits, along with the documentation you will need, we recommend a few more steps so you are mission prepared for your interview with the Social Security Administration claims representative when you apply for your benefits:

- Write down any questions you have on your benefits or how the process works that are still unanswered.

- Print out your Social Security Statement from the Social Security Administration website. Go to www.ssa.gov and click on the link *"Get Your Social Security Statement Online".*

- Write down the names of your spouse(s) and ex-spouse(s) in order of most recent. Next to those name(s), write down the date the marriage started and when it ended. Finally, next to the dates write down (if applicable) how the marriage ended: divorce, death, etc.

- Write down your individual earnings from the most recent year in which you apply for your benefits along with the expected earnings in the year you apply for benefits.

- Gather the necessary original documents to prove your eligibility: Social Security Card, Birth Certificate, your most recent Tax Return and/or earnings statement/W-2, Marriage Certificate (if applicable), Divorce Decree (if applicable), deceased spouse's Death Certificate (if applicable), Military Records (if applicable).

- Bring your personal Social Security Central LLC benefit maximization strategy, generated for you by our proprietary Benefit Maximization Calculator at www.socialsecuritycentral.com.

Finally, you may want to consult with your personal financial professional or tax professional to answer any questions you may have on your Social Security benefits or strategies on how and when to apply. Your financial professional may offer additional guidance on how to maximize your Social Security benefit by having a better understanding of your personal financial situation. Often times, a financial plan will incorporate your Social Security benefits into a strategy that is harmonious with your other financial resources and income. If you feel like your current financial professional or tax professional is not providing you with a strategy that incorporates your Social Security benefits into your retirement income plan or does not have a sufficient understanding of Social Security benefits to maximize your cumulative lifetime benefits, consider interviewing a few professionals to see who seems best for you and your retirement future. Your Social Security benefits are an important retirement asset and can have a significant impact on your ability to maintain your own personal retirement vision and lifestyle.

Where Do I Find the Social Security Administration?

By Mail:

Social Security Administration
Office of Public Inquiries
Windsor Park Building
6401 Security Blvd.
Baltimore, MD 21235

By Phone:

1-800-772-1213 (TTY 1-800 325-0778)
Operators are available weekdays from 7am to 7pm.
Automated services are available 24 hours, 7 days a week.

Online:

www.ssa.gov

In person:

Find a local office at https://secure.ssa.gov/apps6z/FOLO/fo001.jsp.

ABOUT THE AUTHORS

ANGELA S. DEPPE, CPA
DIRECTOR, SOCIAL SECURITY CENTRAL LLC

Angela began her accounting career with Arthur Andersen LLP in Chicago, focusing on tax and compensation planning. Eventually recruited by a consulting firm, she then designed proprietary financial reporting technology solutions for clients. For the past 15 years, Angela designed and consulted on financial, tax, and compensation solutions.

It wasn't until her own mother decided to retire and take her Social Security benefits early at age 62 (losing out on over $100k) that Angela saw the need to educate the baby boomer generation on Social Security. Since starting Social Security Central LLC, Angela developed a proprietary Social Security Benefit Maximization Calculator and co-authored *It's Your Money! Simple Strategies to Maximize Your Social Security Income.*

JOHN D. DEPPE, CMFC
CO-AUTHOR, IT'S YOUR MONEY!

John has spent nearly two decades working for Global Fortune 500 companies and some of the world's largest financial firms including Kemper Funds and ING. For years, John saw a gap in Social Security and retirement income education. He started providing seminars for financial professionals and their clients. Widening his scope, John looked to give everyone a simple, central resource explaining when and how to collect Social Security income. John has helped his wife, Angela, develop Social Security maximization strategies culminating in a proprietary Benefit Maximization Calculator, and co-authored the book *It's Your Money! Simple Strategies to Maximize Your Social Security Income..*

Made in the USA
San Bernardino, CA
25 October 2013